Systems Thinking and Decision Making in Urban and Environmental Planning

Systems Thinking and Decision Making in Urban and Environmental Planning

Anastássios Perdicoúlis

Engineering Department, UTAD, Portugal,
CITTA Research Centre, FEUP, Portugal, and
Oxford Institute for Sustainable Development, OBU, UK

Edward Elgar
Cheltenham, UK • Northampton, MA, USA

Published by
Edward Elgar Publishing Limited
The Lypiatts
15 Lansdown Road
Cheltenham
Glos GL50 2JA
UK

Edward Elgar Publishing, Inc.
William Pratt House
9 Dewey Court
Northampton
Massachusetts 01060
USA

A catalogue record for this book
is available from the British Library

Library of Congress Control Number: 2010929040

Mixed Sources
Product group from well-managed
forests and other controlled sources
www.fsc.org Cert no. SA-COC-1565
© 1996 Forest Stewardship Council
FSC

ISBN 978 1 84980 384 7

Printed and bound by MPG Books Group, UK

Contents

Preface

This is not the first time that systems thinking appears in the planning literature. Rather than replicating previous efforts, this book updates and reinforces them in a special approach featuring extended mental models and descriptive causal diagrams. The guiding vision is 'thoughtfully elaborated plans, communicated properly', distilled from more than twenty years of work, learning, teaching, and experimenting in (and across) a number of fields – for instance urban and regional planning, environmental planning, and system dynamics.

The book brings a fresh approach and material to systems thinking for the planners who are already familiar with it, an attempt to direct the enduring group of adherents away from non-explicit and non-systems modes of planning, and guidance for the young planners, new to systems thinking. The case studies are based on real plans, presented here with a hidden identity so they can be dissected, commented, and reconstructed to protect the reputation of the professionals involved.

The style of the writing is explicative, so younger readers feel guided and welcome. The occasional reference to keywords in Greek and Latin are meant to provide insight into basic notions, again intended mostly for the younger readers. The older and more experienced readers should find enough challenge in the book, for instance with the formality regarding the conception and expression of mental models, as well as the 'systems definition' of the planning problem.

Acknowledgements

The foremost expression of gratitude is to my father who first taught me to think of systems – structure, function, and control – starting with easy mechanical and electrical constructions, and progressively extending to the more abstract social and philosophical realms. I also feel fortunate to have had school and college curricula full of science, philosophy, and art. I wish to extend my thanks to the wider 'systems thinking' and 'planning' communities of academics and practitioners for having paved the way so far, and for keeping an eye open for the future.

Regarding the writing of the book, first I wish to thank my family for their support. Most of this work was developed at Oxford Brookes University (OBU), and I am grateful that it was concluded under an OBU sponsorship. I wish to thank my friends at OBU for their encouragement and fruitful debates. I am also grateful to the administration of my home university, the University of Trás-os-Montes and Alto Douro (UTAD) in Vila Real, Portugal, for having always granted me physical mobility and research autonomy. I am hopeful that this book will provide the basis for more work at my new research base in Portugal, the Faculty of Engineering of the University of Porto (FEUP). I also wish to thank the Portuguese Foundation for Science and Technology (FCT) for having sponsored my 2005–2006 sabbatical year in Oxford, when all this material began to come together.

Finally, I have a special appreciation for the publishing team at Edward Elgar, for being so friendly, efficient, and always available.

1. Introduction

1.1 Motivation and Setting

It is somewhat surprising that important operations such as the conception and testing of action proposals such as development plans or investment projects are, more often than not, carried out mentally – that is, without a written record to get back to, or to share with others. This shortcoming is compensated (whether intentionally or by coincidence) by a plethora of information accompanying the action proposals – for example abundant text, tables (or spreadsheets) and charts, statistics, and geographic maps.

But one can still not connect this information in a way to identify logical or physical sequences of how changes are thought to take place and events to develop. This pattern can be verified in almost every plan published, and many do get widely disseminated through the internet nowadays. It seems to be today's custom, or the way to prepare and present plans, and as such it establishes the example – παράδειγμα or paradigm – for further practice in a kind of a reinforcing loop (Figure 1.1).

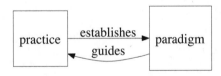

Figure 1.1   *The 'practice–paradigm' process loop: collective practice establishes a paradigm, and this paradigm guides new practice*

Reinforcing loops like the one of Figure 1.1 are difficult to start and equally difficult to stop. If the practice is good (for instance, with a sound methodology), this reinforcement is welcome, as small deviations from the paradigm will not be able to cause significant impacts on the collective practice, and thus practice will continue to be good. On the other hand, though, if the paradigm has taken a wrong direction (for instance, with procedural omissions), then it will most likely misdirect the whole practice and, equally to the previous case, there will be no way of stopping it. Pointing out global wrongdoings or amending global paradigms is a difficult and brave task, with little chance of success. But it is also a duty of those who have observed it – and hence a motivation for this book.

In summary, three major concerns – or inconveniences – arise with the non-explicit style of planning: (a) reasoning is not disclosed, and practically nothing gets revealed about how the proposed solutions were discovered, how they relate to the defined objectives, how the particular objectives were defined, or which specific information was used as references to define the objectives; (b) the proposed action is not followed in cause-and-effect pathways until its intended outcomes, so it is not clear whether or not it will be effective (that is, produce the intended results), or efficient (produce these results without much waste); (c) the selection and fixing of the most appropriate action is not clearly explained in a 'technical' manner, but is often justified as a 'political' way of decision making – Figure 1.2.

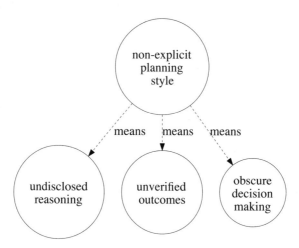

Figure 1.2   The three major concerns (or inconveniences) of non-explicit styles of planning

Yet, there is plenty of room for explicit thought and communication in spatial planning. It is possible to present action proposals in relation to their upstream and downstream elements, such as the objectives and the likely outcomes, respectively. It is also possible to present how the object of a planning effort (that is, the system we aim to modify) is composed and functions independently as well as together with our expectations and intervention (as an 'extended system'), and all this can be shared and debated instead of remaining a private and closed mental model such as a 'black box' – or a number of black boxes, one in each person's mind.

Besides being possible, explicit communication in planning is also necessary. The origin and the prospect of a proposed action should be explained clearly so that the complete idea can be understood, verified, communicated, and optimised. This explanation can be personal, as a way of verifying one's own thoughts, can involve the stakeholders, or those with interest to participate, or can involve anyone such as the community, authorities, academics, or journalists. This effort for better planning marks a deviation from mainstream practice, which is not to be taken lightheartedly. It requires conviction for the purpose, thinking anew, dominating new techniques, searching and acquiring new information, and not minding open debates about assumptions and reasoning. Like all investments, it needs some extra work and persistence in the beginning; then the effort becomes less, and the returns begin to appear: worthy action proposals.

Perhaps an explicative style of planning is not appealing to all planners. Being not the mainstream thinking, people may find it unusual – and it is. But it points to an interesting and challenging direction: clear thinking and communication. The book welcomes new planners into a new kind of thinking and communication, provides methods and techniques for those who appreciate and actively seek clear or transparent thinking, and challenges those who follow today's non-explicit planning paradigm without questioning.

1.2 Workflow and Structure

The book develops from concerns to aims, to original innovations, and finally to applications that mitigate the original concerns. This section provides an overview of the book structure and content. Figure 1.3 illustrates the workflow of the book, created as a descriptive causal diagram (DCD) – see Chapter 4 for the conventions that permit reading this diagram in a technical manner.

In Figure1.2 we saw the three major inconveniences of non-explicit styles of planning: undisclosed reasoning, unverified outcomes, and obscure decision making. The resolution of the first two concerns, undisclosed reasoning and unverified outcomes, requires explicit causal reasoning and expression: how we perceive causality can take planners from static world views (using un-related indicators and 'diagnostic' snapshots such as SWOT, for instance) to dynamic world images with cause-and-effect relationships. The resolution of obscure decision making requires an appropriate learning model, as well as an appropriate definition of the planning problem: learning models indicate how information flows in the planning process and influences everything from the conception of the action to decision making; problems can be defined in a proper systems thinking framework, and pass from mere expressions of pre-occupation or inconvenience to functional and solvable configurations. These three resolutions constitute the aims of the book, and are explored in Chapter 3.

The aims of the book lead to three original innovations or methodological contributions. The first contribution is a planning method based on a special configuration of the planning problem. Because this method features uncom-mon explanations and promotes causal thinking, let us call it 'explicative causal thinking' (ECT). ECT is particularly concerned about causality, from the logic of the problem configuration to the elements of the problem and their relation-ships. Secondly, ECT is assisted by two types of special diagrams, to which we also give equally self-explanatory names: descriptive causal diagrams (DCD) and concise process diagrams (CPD). DCDs constitute a type of causal di-agrams that helps express the four semantics categories of causality: system elements, action, cause-and-effect relationships, and effects. CPDs constitute a compatible and complementary type of diagrams, created for the purpose of presenting processes. Finally, as some action proposals come already pre-pared, we design a special verification method: the diagrammatic causal anal-ysis (DCA). This is a causal analysis technique used to search for causality consistency or errors. DCA is assisted by descriptive causal diagrams (DCD), and has a valuable contribution in assessment processes, such as environmental impact assessment (EIA) and strategic environmental assessment (SEA).

The innovations produced in the book are applied to a number of case stud-

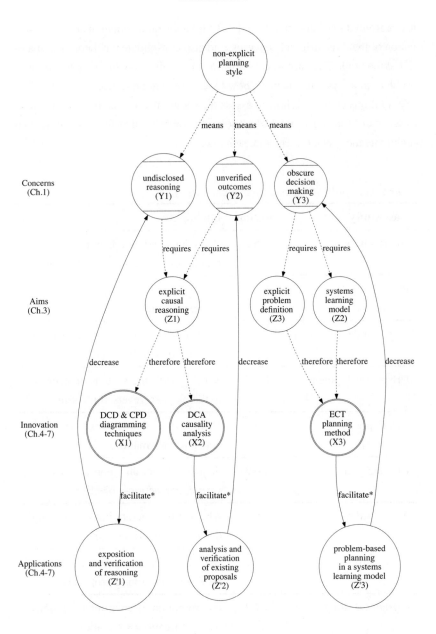

Figure 1.3   The book develops from concerns to aims, to original innovations, and finally to applications that mitigate the original concerns

ies, presented in Chapters 5, 6, and 7. These applications demonstrate the mitigation of the three original concerns, and also consolidate the theoretical material of the book. The case studies illustrate, inter alia, how to focus and define a problem in a 'systems manner', how to ask the 'right questions', how to identify solutions creatively, how to assess the solutions for effectiveness, and how to set up criteria and select the best solution. Table 1.1 lists the case studies and highlights the special interest in each one.

Table 1.1   Applications and their highlights

Case study	Section	Highlights
Home safety	§ 5.2	Procedure to create new plans; exploration of ideas; qualitative simulation.
Personal protection	§ 5.3	Alternative solutions; tiers of outcomes; decision criteria.
Regional development	§ 5.4	Drill down action (tiering); spatial issues; problem definition.
Urban development	§ 5.5	Starting with the system; information to the planner; reverse blueprints.
Health policy	§ 6.2	Drill down action (tiering); abstract to concrete information.
Housing plan	§ 6.3	Sequential action (non-alternatives); verification action–objective.
Arts strategy	§ 6.4	Abstract to concrete information; hidden action; interpretation.
Hydrocarbon pollution	§ 7.1	Text mark-up; process view; causal view; reconditioning proposals.
Offshore drilling	§ 7.2	Incorporation of environmental objectives; mitigation; simulation.
Local transport plan	§ 7.3	Forecasting; action to outcomes; outcomes to action.

The scope of applications in this book, narrowed down through the 'interest filter' of urban and environmental planning, addresses primarily a readership of spatial planners – for example urban and regional planners, such as geographers, civil engineers, and architects, as well as environmental planners, including impact assessment practitioners – who can all learn to become 'systems' planners.

As exposed above, the pathway from concerns to aims to innovation seems necessary (Figure 1.4). A reaction to the situation is essential, otherwise we stand pathetically staring at (or even ignoring) the concerns arising from non-explicit planning.

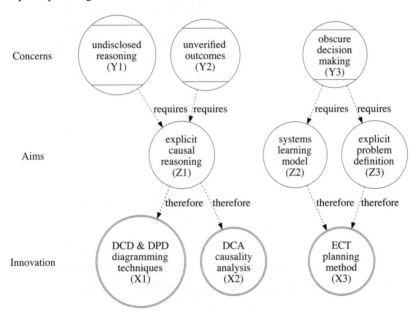

Figure 1.4   Innovations are necessary to achieve the aims, and aims are necessary to resolve the concerns

However, the innovation and applications presented in this book provide no guarantee that planning will necessarily become transparent (Figure 1.5). Starting with the innovation, it may not be understood or applied properly to subsequent case studies. A number of other human factors may reduce the take-up of the methods presented here, such as people's inertia or convenience in the ways they already think and work.

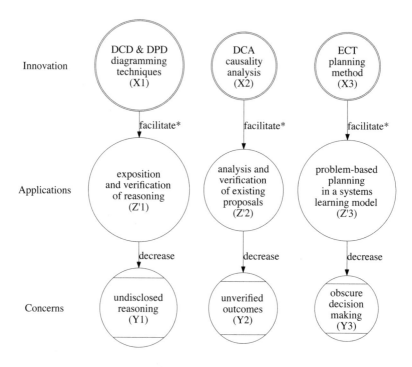

Figure 1.5   There is no guarantee that the innovations will always be applied well, which means that there is also no guarantee that the applications will always mitigate the initial concerns

This book presents an effort to bring a new version of systems thinking to urban and environmental planning – compared to that of the 1970s – as a necessary condition for transparent, easily understandable and communicable planning: to explain how the plans were conceived, how they are expected to achieve their objectives, and how the decision is made. Although it has no guaranteed returns, the effort is worthwhile because it is a step in the right direction.

1.3   Scope and Content

More often than not, urban and environmental planning are associated with map exhibits – whether descriptive of the current situation or normative regarding how certain features should be arranged in space and where activities should take place. Space, and more specifically land, is indeed of prime importance: this is where we live, work, build, sell, buy, etc. One of the milestone planning documents in the UK, the 1947 *Town and Country Planning Act*, defined development plans as 'indicating the manner in which a local planning authority propose that land in their area should be used' (HMSO, 1947, p.4). Development itself is – metaphorically and literally – based on land, as 'the carrying out of building, engineering, mining or other operations in, on, over or under land, or the making of any material change in the use of any buildings or other land' (Cullingworth and Nadin, 1994, p.80). It is not surprising, therefore, that the European Commission adopted the term 'spatial planning' to refer generically to the way each EU member state manages development (European Commission, 1997). But it is also noteworthy that spatial planning starts to exhibit considerable formal integration of social, economic, environmental, and infrastructure aspects (European Commission, 1997, p.34), which gives an extension to development towards other dimensions.

The systems approach to spatial planning by McLoughlin (1969) and Chadwick (1971, 1978) considered space as an evolving entity, and coupled the dimension 'time' to space. This is important as the characteristics of space change along time, whether we plan for these changes or they occur as consequences of anthropogenic or 'natural' actions. An overwhelming interest in space may overshadow other important dimensions, and this seems to have been the case up until the 1960s (Taylor, 1998). One of these dimensions that deserve the planners' attention is time, as the dimension along which we notice change, but the major contribution of the systems approach was the attention to the function (that is, operation or work in a particular way) of the system – as opposed to its appearance or physical aspect along time. Attention to function implies seeking an underlying structure responsible for that function, and takes the planner beyond the visible physical elements: to a 'space' where most of the important elements and their interactions are abstract, and thus hidden from physical view – but which can be, for instance, captured in mathematical models. This 'invisible' reality of function becomes difficult to identify, measure, and communicate. Furthermore, when function becomes the prime concern of the planner, then action gains special importance.

Although space and time are undeniably essential to urban and environmental planning, human action is the third important dimension to be considered – and the most abstract of the three. Plans communicate spatial characteristics or norms in the form of maps, and this has a marked medium of expression and thus a strong presence. Time often appears as the independent variable in development patterns, such as in the data series of statistics, and has a strong presence in tables and charts. Action, though, together with its accompanying elements such as motives, vision, and objectives, at best appears in the text of the plans, usually blended with other support information. Lacking a special or recognisable way to mark its presence in equal terms (in some way 'loud and clear') as space and time, action appears to have less importance and/ or receives less opportunity for thought and consideration.

Unusually for what is considered to be the main tradition in spatial planning, the systems thinking approach to planning gives special importance to action. Chadwick, for instance, considered planning as 'a process of human thought and action based on that thought – in point of fact, forethought, thought for the future' (Chadwick, 1978, p.24). Space and time maintain their importance in planning, set the theme, and articulate with action, but action is of prime importance because it comes at an earlier decision order than space and time: it is of interest and makes sense to ask 'where?' and 'when?' only if we know 'what' to do. In a functional and practical approach, McLoughlin considered planning as a kind of 'error-controlled regulation' (McLoughlin, 1969, p.85), starting with the system to be controlled, the intended state or states of the system, deviation from the intended state, and action to keep the system within the desired limits. The position and importance of action in decision making is further explained in the following chapter.

The plans – or to be more exact, 'action proposals' – considered in this book span a variety of application contexts, from federal to local government, and can be hierarchically ordered in tiers – Figure 1.6. For example, policy is at a higher tier, meaning it is more condensed and abstract than plans; in the same way, plans contain less detail than programmes, and so on. This classification is variable in practice, as much in the number of tiers as in the content and the designation (name) of each tier.

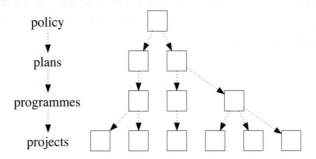

policy

plans

programmes

projects

*Figure 1.6   Hierarchical tiers of action proposals; the objectives correspond-
ing to these proposals can be tiered in a similar way*

This book attempts to explore and document the abstract domain of action
that lies underneath the dynamics – or the forces of change – of development
that manifest in space and time. Great systems thinking contributors to planning such as McLoughlin and Chadwick made an effort in the last decades to
focus on the dynamic aspect of 'change along time' and thus enrich (or maybe
change the course of) the design-based planning practice with the idea of system structure and function. This book goes one step further, focussing on the
'action behind change': the motive force – δύναμις in Greek – in dynamics.

To this end, the book builds some formal expressions to help with the organisation of the information to be processed. The preferred learning model
featuring a special information flow and decision support as well as the conception and formulation of the 'planning problem' in a 'systems way' reveal
preoccupation with structure and function regarding not only the systems of
interest, but also the planning procedure – thus forming an extended system. It
follows that the resolution of the original concerns regarding non-explicit planning, expressed in this book, leads to a higher degree of formality in planning.

The book is intended to be both a textbook for planning students (under-
graduate as well as research) and a handbook for young planning practitioners
(for example town planners, policy makers, EIA/ SEA professionals) who seek
a practical approach to systems thinking and clear, problem-solving reasoning
to orient their practice. Therefore, the book is written in a rather technical style

– as opposed to the typical 'theoretical' style of most planning books – with many examples and illustrations. New and difficult notions are introduced with easy examples, while the content becomes progressively more advanced from the beginning to the end of the book.

2. Systems Thinking

2.1 Overview

Systems thinking has seen many definitions, but let us keep it simple. It is a way of thinking about complex things, and these are generally things that 'work' or 'do something' – let us call them 'systems', meaning a set of connected parts forming a complex whole. Whether natural or human-made, systems often receive the admiration and respect of observers: because they are complex or because they function. For lack of understanding, possibly due to overwhelming information, systems may be greeted by the layperson – or the professional who does not have the time to study them properly – with awe rather than curiosity and patience to explore them. For the sake of simplicity, systems are often considered as 'black boxes' of which we merely know the interfaces: the inputs and the outputs.

Instead of seeing a 'black box' out of every machine, city, or community, systems thinking tends to give a suitable scale and resolution of information and to seek understanding regarding what is in there and how it functions as a unit – that is, an identifiable system. Instead of perceiving and working with isolated indicators of concern, such as national unemployment or an unusual noise in our car, systems thinking prompts us to think of the 'bigger picture' – the country as an economic system or the vehicle as a mechanical system – and then we can effectively start our troubleshooting and plan our intervention. In a sense, systems thinking can be the natural way of thinking of curious people, who are not daunted by the alleged difficulty of the complex object or situation. Instead, it actively confronts complexity, wanting to know and understand how systems are put together and function; leaving no mystery unsolved, and no black box unopened. The requirements are curiosity, time, and some initial knowledge.

For Peter Senge (1990), one of the current systems thinking leaders, systems thinking is more than a way of thinking: it is a discipline – something that can be taught. Systems thinkers see wholes that function rather than input-output transformers; they also see the parts of the whole and the relationships among them; they see patterns of change rather than static snapshots.

A popular operational application of systems thinking, known as system dynamics, was conceived by Jay Forrester in the 1950s and developed actively from the 1960s onwards (Forrester, 1961, 1969, 1971). System dynamics provides a platform to enhance learning in complex systems, to help people learn about dynamic complexity, understand how people think, and design more effective policies. Although system dynamics is best known for its numerical models and simulation, it also features underlying conceptual models – that is, the 'thinking' part as opposed to the 'calculating' part. For John Sterman (2000, p.4), one of the current system dynamics leaders, the development of systems thinking is crucial for the survival of humanity. Systems thinking gives the capacity to people to regard the world as a complex system, in which 'everything is connected to everything else'. Sterman claims that having a systems (also known as 'holistic') worldview, people would have a chance to act in consonance with the long term best interests of the system as a whole – which hints at sustainable development.

In this book we consider three special characteristics of systems thinking: (a) a special way of obtaining and processing information, or a 'systems learning model', (b) an explicit definition of the planning problem, and (c) explicit reasoning regarding causality – or cause and effect relationships. These special characteristics of systems thinking constitute the three aims of the book and are required to resolve the three major inconveniences of non-explicit planning: undisclosed reasoning, unverified outcomes, and obscure decision making – as explained in Chapter 1.

2.2   Historic Background

Systems thinking has existed for many years, although not always known as such. The famous parable of the shadows in the cave, for instance, in *The Republic* (Plato, 360 BC, Book VII), is a lesson of systems thinking at the practical level, as well as of values such as knowledge and education at a higher, more philosophical level. In this parable, the reality of the viewers consists of shadows on the wall of the cave where they live (Figure 2.1).

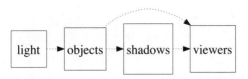

Figure 2.1   Plato's parable as a flow of information: what the viewers see are the shadows of the objects, not the objects themselves

Plato's parable prompts for awareness regarding all the elements involved in producing the obvious reality: the shadows, the original objects, and the light. When important elements are being ignored (for instance, the light, the original objects, as well as the 'mechanism' or 'method' of how shadows are being produced), then thinking is constrained. And thinking is further constrained by peoples' conformism and lack of inquisitiveness – as in the parable their necks are fastened and thus their heads prevented from turning. Encouraging people to seek further knowledge is a deep message for systems thinking: to look beyond the obvious, familiar and convenient; move freely from the seat and seek what produces the shadows; get up and – both literally and metaphorically – see the light.

Let us shift into more recent times, to review the systems thinking ideas among scientists and philosophers across a variety of fields of interest (Figure 2.2), which set the background for the contemporary state of affairs. Just before the 20th C., several russian scientists, such as Bogdanov and Lyapunov, came up with systems ideas which influenced Bertalanffy to form the general systems theory (GST). GST, together with developments from many scientific disciplines, gave rise to systems theory, in which many famous scientists were involved – for instance, Rapoport, Boulding, Ashby, Bateson, and Churchman. By the mid-20th C., new theories and engineering approaches were formed within the same school of thinking, such as cybernetics, control theory, and operations research.

In the meantime, by the beginning of the 20th C., Geddes and Abercrombie were introducing systemic ideas into planning – which along time has come under a variety of designations such as town planning, urban and regional planning, spatial planning, and many more (European Commission, 1997). It was

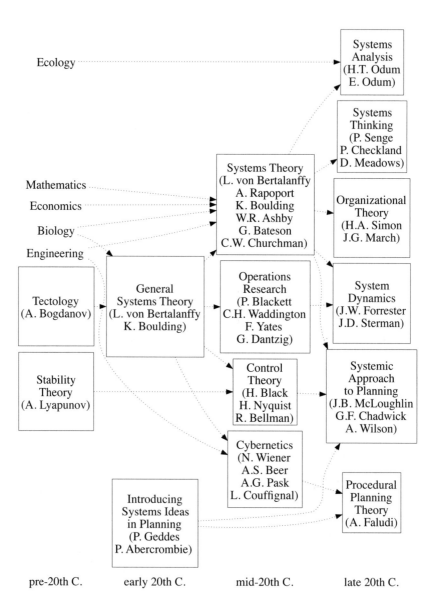

Figure 2.2   Systems scholarship in the 20th C.; while everything potentially links with everything else, only major trends are shown here

only in the second half of the 20th C. that systems thinking in planning received a formal and quite strong incentive, mainly by McLoughlin and Chadwick, at a time when science and engineering were echoing organisational theory, systems analysis, and the early steps of system dynamics. By the end of the 20th C., the term 'systems thinking' was being used mostly by a number of scientists and consultants in the field of business management and organisational learning.

The introduction of systems thinking into planning by the 1970s brought in notions of information theory, control, modelling, and simulation. Most of these ideas, being at an experimental stage and carefully isolated on the 'technical side of planning', were indeed breaking new ground and were often greeted as such. But they were introduced at a time when the required information technology was not widely accessible, and when systems control engineering applications were not so prominent. These early efforts did not get everything right immediately, either. Some of the early proposals, which were mostly 'fruit of their times', were quite polarised – for instance, the plan evaluation method 'cost-benefit analysis' (CBA) had a tendency to convert everything to money, and this soon caused strong reactions as being too simplistic or inadequate for a number of variables such as happiness and human dignity. As another example, linear programming was conceptually accessible, but simply not adequate for non-linear systems – even with the best sets of fitting assumptions. Because the technical means were not there yet, and because the ideas were somewhat still in their first versions, the early efforts to bring systems thinking into planning practically failed to make a permanent mark in the planning paradigm. And with them, the main message of the effort was also lost: to think of systems, structure and function.

2.3 Major Contributions

Now let us take a closer look at the important contributions of systems thinking in relation to planning, and how these provide the foundation material for developing the aims set in this book (§ 1.2).

2.3.1 Systems Planning

For having given formality, focus, and practical orientation to the work and ideas of a number of systems thinkers before them, Brian McLoughlin and George Chadwick can be considered the 'systems pioneers' in spatial planning. Their work developed in parallel, with mutual credits but no common publication. Their ideas started to appear in publications from the 1960s (Chadwick, 1966) to the 1970s (McLoughlin, 1969; Chadwick, 1971, 1978), and some even in the 1980s (Chadwick, 1987). Both authors have been concerned with the understanding of the structure and behaviour of urban and regional systems, not only to study how these change but also how they might be changed.

The influences of McLoughlin and Chadwick came from the direction of the general systems theory (GST), operations research (OR), and cybernetics, and people such as Stafford Beer, Chapin, and Webber. Advances in decision making, such as linear programming, were released in the post World War II era, and caught the attention of both authors. At the same time there were also planning practice innovations demonstrating that the city could, indeed, be interpreted as a kind of system – as, for instance, Mitchell and Rapkin demonstrated with the Detroit and Chicago transportation studies as early as 1954 (McLoughlin, 1969, p.80). As McLoughlin expressed them, the benefits of a systems view in planning were considered to be (a) a single framework of the planning process, in which stakeholders may interact, and (b) a single view of the city, to see better the extent of problems and opportunities. The main downside was considered to be uncertainty due to complexity of large systems.

Systems were central to the classic work of McLoughlin and Chadwick, and were considered as 'sets of objects together with relationships between the objects and between their attributes' (Chadwick, 1978, p.36, citing Hall and Fagen). In addition to systems, or the 'real world', McLoughlin defined the images or mental models of systems to be 'not the real world, but a way of looking at it' (McLoughlin, 1969, p.79).

The way planners acquire knowledge about the system they intend to modify is reflected in the planning process – that is the way they proceed to collect and process information, and we will consider this in detail in § 3.2. In McLoughlin's planning process, for instance, the 'environment' – which is the target system – is 'scanned' to produce an explicit mental model, which is essential for a more profound systems learning (Figure 2.3). The presence of the mental model is a fundamental feature in systems thinking ways of planning.

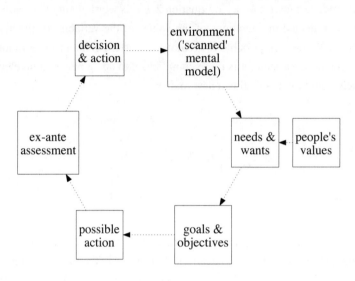

Figure 2.3   Information flow in McLoughlin's planning process

Being realistic, both McLoughlin and Chadwick considered evolution in their target systems: a progressive change through time, much of which could be prepared for – that is, planned. In fact, the recommended form of plans for both authors is statements that prescribe how the city (system) should evolve in a series of equal steps – for instance, in five-year intervals.

Describing systems in mathematical terms was considered to give some desirable precision, which would subsequently allow mathematical processing of the information. After obtaining the necessary information, for instance through a survey, a system could first be described statically, at any point in time, by a vector that represented a list of variables – each variable with its own value – such the vector v in Equation 2.1.

$$v = \begin{bmatrix} a_n \\ b_n \\ \vdots \\ z_n \end{bmatrix} \qquad (2.1)$$

Restoring realism in the description of the system, the state of the system along time could be represented as a time series of vectors like the above. This would produce a matrix M, as in Equation 2.2. It is worth noting that evolution in time is reflected in alterations of the values of the variables of the system matrix M. While it is possible to 'remove' a system element by assigning a zero value to its variable, it is more complicated to add a new system element – which would imply creating a new matrix.

$$M = \begin{bmatrix} a_n & a_{n+1} & \cdots & a_\infty \\ b_n & b_{n+1} & \cdots & b_\infty \\ \vdots & \vdots & & \vdots \\ z_n & z_{n+1} & \cdots & z_\infty \end{bmatrix} \qquad (2.2)$$

Space could also be expressed in mathematical terms, and particularly spatial interactions in the form of equations. For instance, the 'demographic force of attraction' was conceived to be analogous to that of gravitational force of attraction in Newtonian physics, as shown in Example 2.1.

Example 2.1   Force of attraction

$$F = \frac{N_1 N_2}{d^2}$$

where:

- F is the force of attraction
- N_1 and N_2 are two objects, such as two groups of people, at a distance d apart

---

Influenced by the then very popular linear programming techniques, both authors present the planning objectives in mathematical formulas known as 'objective functions'. For instance, Example 2.2 defines an objective function and accompanying information, with the intention (objective) to minimise the value of the function.

Example 2.2   Objective function

Minimise:

$$f = \sum_{all\ i} \sum_{all\ j} d_{ij} x_{ij}$$

subject to:

$$\sum_i x_{ij} = E_j$$

$$\sum_j x_{ij} = W_i$$

$$x_{ij} \geq 0$$

where:

- x_{ij} is the number of people who live in zone i and work in zone j
- d_{ij} is the distance from i to j
- E_j represents the total employment in zone j
- W_i represents the workers in residential zone i

Chadwick's definition of the planning problem (Equation 2.3) reveals the same idea as the objective function (Chadwick, 1978, p.124).

$$\text{Problem} = \text{Goal} + \text{Impediment to that Goal} \tag{2.3}$$

McLoughlin (1969, p.120, citing Bor) admits that it takes time, patience and understanding to clarify the objectives, or what is intended to be achieved, highlighting the dialogue between all the people involved – including the planners and politicians. The solution to an 'objective function' type of problem is a range of values for a number of variables. This was in accordance with the control conception of a system, where the action of the planner would be to adjust the values of a number of variables according to the solution. This also fits the idea of Chadwick and McLoughlin that plans were projected future states of the system, which were to be achieved by adjusting the right variables. The 'adjustment action', though, works only with existing systems and cannot easily account for new elements in the system – as would be, for instance, with a new action that would restructure the system instead of adjusting its parameters.

In the first systems books of planning, the modelling of the systems was done in mathematical terms, all in equations – for instance, traffic models, market models, etc. This was giving an 'exact science' aspect to planning, and was probably discouraging people who did not like mathematics. System modelling was very crude, though, with gross simplifications about (non-)linearity, perhaps appealing only to the mathematically inclined, and difficult to apply by non-technically oriented planners. But, at an age where computers were not very accessible, forecasting was achieved mostly by solving sets of equations manually, using mathematical and graphical methods. Computer simulation was so appealing that at the first opportunity Chadwick experimented with Forrester's system dynamics modelling and simulation techniques (see § 2.3.2).

The assessment of plans had both qualitative and quantitative aspects. Both McLoughlin and Chadwick used plan assessment techniques that were popular at the time, such as cost–benefit analysis, which introduced monetary considerations into the objective functions. Variations of the cost–benefit were also sought, such as Lichfield's 'planning balance sheet' method or Hill's 'goals–achievement' matrix. In a qualitative way, for instance, McLoughlin (1969) examined plans following four predominant aspects: (a) activity – 'Is the type of activity proposed consistent with the intentions of the plan, such as residential, recreational, etc.?'; (b) space – 'Is the amount of space proposed consistent with the plan, such as floor area, parking spaces, etc.?'; (c) communications – 'Is the amount of communications proposed consistent with the plan, such as the numbers of trips..., etc.?'; (d) channels – 'Is this type of channel consistent with the plan, such as the 400 kV overhead cables, dual two-lane limited access road, etc.?'

2.3.2   System Dynamics

System dynamics typically takes a quantitative approach to systems thinking. The popularity of system dynamics is perhaps due to the facility it gives to numerical simulations through the use of stock-and-flow diagrams (SFD), with the use of special software. This is appreciated by anyone who wants to have numerical models of their systems, and most importantly make use of the nu-

merical data regarding the current situations, as well as have numerical forecasts for the outcomes of their plans.

But besides the numerical models expressed in mathematical equations and
their graphical interface of stock-and-flow diagrams (SFD), system dynamics
also uses conceptual models – and many system dynamicists will defend that
one should start with the concepts. The conceptual models in system dynamics
are known as causal loop diagrams (CLD), and contain qualitative information
about the system elements and their causal relationships, as well as about the
feedback loops observed in the system. These are closer to systems thinking
than the numerical models.

The causal relationships between elements are marked with labelled arrows.
An arrow label such as a '+' sign (for instance in Figure 2.4) attributes a relative meaning to change: it does not indicate an increase, but a change in the
'same direction' as the change of the other element upstream. To avoid a potential confusion of the relative '+' or '−' signs with absolute increase or
decrease, some people prefer the alternative (but still relative) marking set of
's/o', meaning the 'same' or the 'other' direction of change, respectively.

CLDs also determine and label the type of the feedback loops: for instance,
a ⌒−↴or ⌒B↴label inside a loop indicates a negative or balancing (stabilising)
feedback loop, while a ⌒+↴ or ⌒R↴ label indicates a positive or reinforcing
feedback loop. Let us consider Figure 2.4 to illustrate an example of a positive
feedback loop captured in a very simple CLD. An elevated car use in a city or
country poses an apparent need for more roads, and this is manifested in the
direction from right to left. On the other hand, more roads facilitate (or even
invite) the use of more cars – manifested in the direction from left to right.
Repeating these changes in a sequence, the result of this positive feedback is
something like a city or a country full of cars and roads.

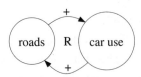

*Figure 2.4   An example of a simple causal loop diagram; the + signs mark
the arrows, while the 'R' symbol marks the feedback loop*

A positive feedback loop like the above has more links with reality, such as conditions (upstream) or consequences (downstream). For instance, conditions can be the capacity of the city or country residents to invest in the purchase of cars, or the availability of fuel to run these cars. Consequences can be a boost to the economy, such as the auto industry and associated services – for instance petrol stations, auto repairs, and road services. The amount and the type of information to represent in the diagram reflects the mental model of the planning team regarding the particular case of interest.

Although CLDs convey very useful information to planners, they have one major shortcoming for the purpose: the effects are expressed as relative changes. What planners really want to see are the likely effects in absolute terms – whether as facts (for example 'increase') or evaluations (for example 'improvement'). This shortcoming provides a motivation and an opportunity for an innovation presented in Chapter 4, namely the creation of the descriptive causal diagrams (DCD) that describe the effects as absolute changes.

2.3.3   Soft Systems Methodology

Soft systems methodology (SSM) was developed in the 1970s based on systems engineering approaches, primarily by Peter Checkland and others (Checkland, 1981; Checkland and Scholes, 1990; Checkland and Holwell, 1998). The primary use of SSM was in the analysis of complex situations where there are divergent views about the definition of the problem – 'soft problems' such as 'What to do about homelessness amongst young people?'.

Perhaps one of the greatest contributions of SSM and its developers is an alternative definition of systems. Contrary to what would be 'natural' or thematic divisions, systems are not defined by boundaries or contexts such as the economy, population, and the physical environment, but rather as a custom-made sets defined for the purposes of administration or planning. Therefore, 'soft' systems consist of various elements that have important interactions among them. It becomes difficult to label that system in conventional terminology – for example health, economy, public administration, or agriculture.

The 'classic' SSM consisted of seven steps, while in the 1990s this was condensed to four steps, as illustrated in Figure 2.5 (Checkland, 2000). SSM has always been about problem solving designed for collaborative environments, as opposed to 'desktop' exercises. These interactive environments, with 'live' sessions and explanations, have sustained the use of 'rich pictures' which contain a reduced or relaxed degree of formality – comparing, for instance, with system dynamics models. Rich pictures characterised SSM from its early stages, facilitating 'free expression' with icons, arrows, and text.

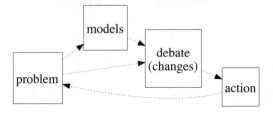

Figure 2.5   The four-step soft systems methodology protocol

The use of explicit and shared mental models is another feature that SSM has developed and sustained. From early on, SSM employed techniques to identify important information about the planning problem, such as the people involved, the processes, and their environment. This was used to prompt thinking about what the entity (for example government, authority, business) was trying to achieve, how the desired change could be achieved, and what would be the best solution.

2.3.4   Strategic Choice Approach

The strategic choice approach (SCA) appeared by the end of the 1960s, developed by John Friend, Neil Jessop, and later Allen Hickling as an ongoing process in which the planned management of uncertainty plays a crucial role (Friend and Hickling, 2005). SCA was designed to be collaborative and highly interactive, with documentation being a key feature of the communication among the team members, hence SCA features many types of diagrams with versatile and non-standardised expressions – more than in the case of SSM (§ 2.3.3).

The SCA process features four 'hubs' that process the problem and help produce a final decision – Figure 2.6. While the typical entry of the problem is the 'shaping' hub and the typical exit is the 'choosing' hub, SCA is characterised by its little adherence to a fixed process protocol. The freedom and flexibility to proceed is understandable in the context of highly interactive environments where SCA has its applications.

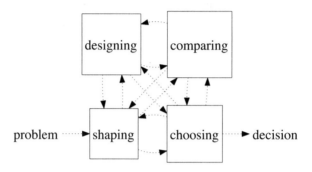

Figure 2.6   The strategic choice approach protocol

SCA appears to be the dominant 'strategic' text for spatial planners, counting since the 1970s. SCA is considered as a 'soft OR' (Operational Research) approach, while OR's typical concern with 'strategic planning' has been directed mostly towards industrial or commercial applications. Although based on a systemic approach, SCA adopts an incremental and exploratory approach to planning, based on the acknowledgement of an unstable, uncertain background characterised by multiple actors and rationales.

2.3.5   Strategy Maps

Many systems thinking academics and consultants have turned their attention to the business sector, with strong presences such as Peter Senge and Russel Ackoff. System dynamics has had a remarkable reception there, not so much due to its qualitative conceptual models but rather due to its facility with numerical simulation. For those who still appreciate a succinct qualitative overview of the structure and function of a system such as an enterprise, Kaplan and Norton have contributed with an increasingly popular method known as 'strategy maps' (Kaplan and Norton, 2000, 2004a,b).

Robert Kaplan and David Norton developed strategy maps as a means to illustrate and elaborate an earlier concept, the balanced scorecard (Kaplan and

Norton, 1996). Strategy maps are visual representations of the strategy of an organisation, illustrating the cause-and-effect relationships between different strategic objectives and their measures – Figure 2.7. They constitute yet another manifestation of the diversity of ways that mental models can be captured, expressed and shared.

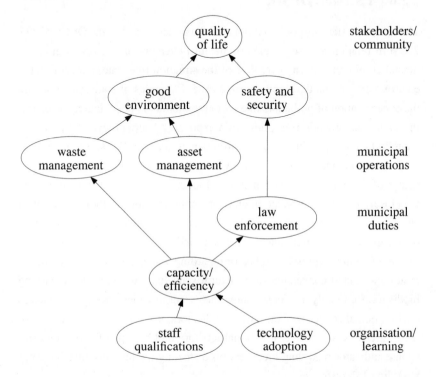

Figure 2.7   Example of a Kaplan-Norton strategy map for the public sector

The Kaplan-Norton (KN) strategy maps became rapidly very popular in the business world, and then extended to non-profit and governmental organisations. Their representational techniques are generally not very rigorous in the expression of causality – for instance, sometimes resulting in ambiguous links. In addition, strategy elements such as objectives or action are not always expressed consistently, which may result in further ambiguity.

Figure 2.7 also illustrates the strong organisational aspect of the Kaplan-Norton strategy maps, namely the four perspectives that constitute the 'backbone' of the maps. Coming from the business sector, these four perspectives are typically financial, customer, internal, and learning and growth – contrast with those of Figure 2.7.

2.3.6 PSR and DPSIR

The 'pressure-state-response' (PSR) model was developed by the OECD (1993, 2003) in relation to a set of environmental indicators. Indicators of environmental conditions give an overview of the situation (the state) concerning the environment and its development over time. Examples of state indicators are the concentration of pollutants in environmental media (state indicator regarding toxic contamination) or population exposure to certain levels of pollution (state indicator regarding urban environmental quality). Pressures are considered to be human activities themselves or the use of resources and the discharge of pollutants and waste materials. Indicators of environmental pressures are closely related to production and consumption patterns; they often reflect emission or resource use intensities, along with related trends and changes over a given period. Examples of pressure indicators are the intensity of use of water resources (pressure indicator regarding water resources) or habitat alteration and land conversion from natural state (pressure indicator regarding biodiversity). Finally, responses show the extent to which society responds to environmental concerns. Examples of indicators of societal responses are protected areas as percentage of national territory and by type of ecosystem (response indicator regarding biodiversity) or fishing quotas (response indicator regarding fish resources).

The PSR model represents interactions between the state of the environment, pressures and responses. The interactions between state and pressure are physical relationships, while any interaction related to the response is based on information (Figure 2.8). Although the choice of the term 'response' may indicate a reactive societal attitude, the 'response' element of the PSR model can very well host 'planning' with a pro-active attitude.

The PSR has served as the base for a number of adjusted versions, one of which is the very popular 'driving force-pressure-state-impact-response' (DPSIR) model used by the European Environment Agency. The DPSIR is frequently expressed as a process model (Figure 2.9), where all five elements are

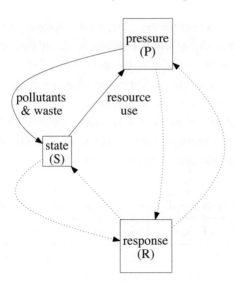

Figure 2.8   The PSR model as a process, with physical and information flows

considered to belong to the same semantic category – see § 4.1 regarding process diagrams.

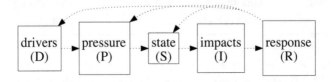

Figure 2.9   The DPSIR model as a process with information flows

2.3.7   SWOT Analysis

SWOT analysis is a technique used in planning to characterise, evaluate, classify, and generally organize the information about the system under development. The SWOT analysis has been very popular among many schools of planning, both in the private and the public sector (Mintzberg et al., 1998). In its most common form, the technique features four semantic categories: strengths, weaknesses, opportunities, and threats. The first two typically refer to the internal conditions (that is, the system of interest), while the other two typically refer to the external conditions – that is, the 'environment' of the system. This requires a very clear idea of what is within and what is outside the system of interest, which often needs very careful thinking.

The information in SWOT analysis is typically organised in four-column tables such as Table 2.1. Although it is based on facts, a SWOT table contains assessed and classified information expressed subjectively.

Table 2.1   SWOT analysis sample from a regional development plan

Strong Points	**Weak Points**	**Opportunities**	**Threats**
Heterogenous landscape and environment	Needs in solid waste deposition sites	Environmentally friendly tourism dynamics	Crisis in agriculture, generating less respect to the environment
Satisfactory evolution in solid waste collection	Insufficient primary school network in the urban centers	Commercial potential of the mineral waters and spas	Open landfills create risks to public health and detract from the region's profile

Being very popular as the starting or reference point for many planning efforts, SWOT analysis often serves as the base for finding direct solutions regarding action – for instance solutions to the identified weak points, or ideas for enhancement of the opportunities. Although this may appear as a good idea, it creates shortcuts that condition the decision making – as we will see in § 3.2.

2.3.8   Effect Matrices

Effect (or impact) matrices were used extensively in the 1970s, at the beginning of the environmental impact assessment (EIA) methodology, for their capacity to explicitly relate information: on one hand the components of action (typically investment projects), and on the other components of the system that would receive the project. The crossing of the two arrays of information allows space to mark the likely effects (that is changes or 'impacts', as they were known in earlier applications of the technique) of the proposed action on the system. The advantage of this type of matrix is the fine resolution with which information is displayed, processed, and forecast – Table 2.2.

Table 2.2   Generic structure of an effect matrix

	Component 1	**Component 2**	**Component 3**
Action A	Effect A1	Effect A2	Effect A3
Action B	Effect B1	Effect B2	Effect B3
Action C	Effect C1	Effect C2	Effect C3

The information contained in an effect matrix such as Table 2.2 can be represented in an alternative way, for instance as a directed graph – also known as a 'digraph'. Figure 2.10 represents the system components as numbers (1–3) and the proposed actions as letters (A–C). The effects (A1–C3) are marked on the arrows that represent the causal relationships.

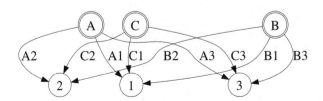

Figure 2.10   The information of an effect matrix can be represented as a directed graph

Both the effect matrices and their equivalent digraphs can reach large dimensions, in which cases they can become quite complex. One of the simplification techniques from the matrix side is partial completion – that is, representing only the effects considered as 'significant' – while one of the techniques coming from the digraph side is the spatial ordering of the graph elements – as we will see in several examples in this book.

2.4 Conclusion

This brief review of systems thinking gave us a panorama of developments and the current state of affairs regarding the specific application of planning. In the following chapter we can start deepening on the main aspects of systems thinking for planning, under the umbrella heading of 'decision making'.

3. Decision Making

3.1 Overview

Decision has many interpretations and definitions. The basic notion is quite crude: it is practically a 'cut-off' operation – from Latin *de-* (off) and *caedere* (to cut). Most of the time 'decision' is used metaphorically, to indicate a selection of an option by severing or eliminating all the others. The important highlight of the metaphor is the irreversibility of the selection, which makes the decision final. During any process, such as planning, there are a number of decisions to be made and they are all important because each one eliminates possible options – for instance development pathways. In every process there is always a special decision, though, and that is typically by the conclusion of the process. A conclusive process has a clear answer for questions such as 'So, what do we do?', and that is the product of the final decision.

In planning, as in many other professional activities, decision is considered as the most valued, appreciated, or important part. Decision makers occupy the top ranks of professions and typically issue (or at least shape) the orders for action, or what is to be done. There are many qualities to be appreciated in decision makers, such as leadership, judgement, and other personal capacities and skills, but there is one external quality considered crucial: the decision maker must be informed.

To understand what an 'informed' decision means, let us approximate the way decisions are made. In general terms, the information required for selecting the best option has two sources: (a) the available options, for instance regarding action, and (b) the criteria for the selection, which express what we intend to achieve by the particular decision (Figure 3.1). While the decision maker can operate with these two elements, the preparation of these elements probably exceeds the jurisdiction of the basic 'decision making'.

The decision maker as a selector should be sufficiently informed by the available options for action and the selection criteria, but the information that

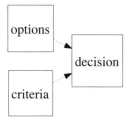

Figure 3.1   Decision making requires knowledge of the available options and relevant criteria

reaches the decision maker is quite simple or superficial. For a more thorough examination of the options and the criteria, let us shift one level up and move to the preparation level, which contains a greater amount of information – this is an opportunity to find out more. In some cases (especially in planning contexts) this is considered as an extended function of the decision maker.

The preparation phase contains a grand volume of information that becomes processed and channeled to decision making both as options and as criteria, and this information must be processed appropriately: with care, creativity, and respect for the references – for instance, facts and assumptions. The importance of the preparation phase is perhaps best given by an expression of information technology that describes the risk of handling the information to reach the decision stage, and that is known as 'GIGO': garbage in, garbage out. This has two interpretations for decision making, regarding the action options and the decision criteria respectively: (a) 'with no good options on offer, the decision cannot be good', and (b) 'the wrong rules will pick up the wrong options'. If errors are introduced at the preparation stages, such as inappropriate action options or irrelevant selection rules, then the decision maker risks malpractice either by judging with the wrong criteria or by picking up an inappropriate option.

Decision is appreciated for respecting its options and rules (or criteria). While creativity is welcome in the discovery of the 'options', it is generally not appreciated in the act of deciding. There are two famous exceptions, though: the selected option of Alexander the Great to solve the Gordian knot by cutting it, and of Columbus to crush the egg's tip so it can stand upright. As the selected options of both men responded to their respective objectives, they were valid decisions and managed to produce the intended outcomes – although somewhat forcefully or inelegantly. Other than these two examples, disrespecting the decision rules and/or the options is not a good idea. For instance, in the ancient Greek theatre, and in subsequent interpretations, there was an occasional divine intervention presented through a God delivered on stage with the help of a mechanical construction: a crane or 'machine' (μηχανή). This practice became widely known in subsequent years through its Latin translation, *Deus ex Machina*, and was used to produce a solution to the plot (for instance dilemmas) that was unrelated to the play until then. This was (a) introducing completely new options unexpectedly, and (b) using a divine status to make the selection of the newly introduced option, over-riding the standard decision rules of the humans. Whether or not this is a reality of the so called 'political scene' it will not be of concern in this technical book.

In the next sections we shall meet and explore the three aims of this book. The flow of information to support decision making is crucial, and § 3.2 examines a number of learning models before designing a suitable option for planning: the systems learning model. § 3.3 provides insights about causal relationships and strengthens explicit causal reasoning. In order to get meaningful solutions we must learn how to formulate problems appropriately, and § 3.4 shows how to set up explicitly and solve the planning problems in a special way of systems thinking.

3.2   Information Flow Models

As we saw in the previous section, the decision maker obtains information and functions in two modes: (a) as the creator or producer of the action options and the selection criteria, and/or (b) as the selector of the most appropriate option according to the selection criteria. These two modes are well known in cognitive psychology and related applications – for instance, as 'single loop' and 'double loop' learning, respectively (Argyris, 1985; Sterman, 2000). In a simple explanation, the decision maker can learn (or be informed) through one or two types of information: (a) the facts, such as events and/or data – for instance, an accident on Motorway 5, and three injured people – and (b) the causes that produced these events or data – for instance slippery road surface, driver distraction, or vehicle malfunction. For some decisions, only the first type (or level) of information is required – for instance, in order to calculate and decide how many ambulance vehicles to dispatch. For other decisions, for instance to attribute liability, both levels of information are required.

From the reception of facts and/or causal explanations until the decision for action (or no action), information flows in a number of ways – or 'information flow models'. The various information flow models, which include the processing of information, can account for better (for instance, 'learned') or worse (for instance, rash) decisions. Since in systems thinking we want to 'see' everything that is not visible with the eyes, let us take a closer look at these models.

3.2.1   The Data Learning Model

In the first model of learning the acquired knowledge is simple: facts or data. The learning entity is informed of the state of affairs and considers what to do in reaction to that. The decision about the action to take is made against selection rules. Let us consider an example and produce an illustration to trace the information flows (Figure 3.2). Traffic jams are known to take place 'globally' (system), and specific information reaches the learning entity (for instance, the transport department) that there are several cases of particularly severe traffic jams in important places (status data). The learning entity immediately starts thinking what to do (options) against traffic jams, which most likely involves a review of known solutions, and will select one or more of the options that are considered effective (rule). By adopting the right measures, the learning entity expects to reduce a number of traffic jams, which is also a contribution against the global condition (system).

The data learning model, whose general pattern is depicted in Figure 3.3, is similar to the planning routines centered around a SWOT analysis. SWOT may point out insufficiencies so we can provide instant relief, and the best option can be selected, for instance, according to effectiveness or available funds. We can coin more names for the data learning model: for instance the 'relief' model, as the main concern is to respond to a crisis; the 'firefighter' model, since the firefighters know what to do when they are informed of a fire; or the 'thermostat' model, as this is exactly what control units (that is, simple regulatory machines) are designed to do.

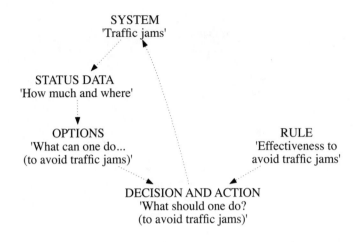

Figure 3.2   Example of the data learning model

3.2.2   The Imprinted Model

The second model of learning has one more degree of complexity. The options for action and the decision rules are generated from a higher level of knowledge – that is, a 'mental model'. As cognitive maps, mental models contain our understanding and knowledge, but also include assumptions and generalisations. Mental models can be thematic: we can have one per theme or subject, such as family, the economy, or politics. Finally, mental models are often dynamic: they explain 'how things work' – in other words, they represent causal connections among entities. In a 'learning' mode, mental models summarise how we see and understand the world, while in a 'decision' mode they influence how we reach conclusions and take action.

Very often we are not aware of our mental models or the effects they have on our behaviour. This is why we say that mental models are 'tacit', which means they are understood or implied without being stated. Mental models are often personal, but can be brought to the surface, shared, and even verified and updated. Theories, for instance, are formal, shared, and generally accepted mental models. A theory – in Greek θεωρία (contemplation, speculation), associated to θεωρός (spectator) – is a 'view' that one or more people receive and save (and perhaps process, or 'personalise') into a mental model, and in the case of

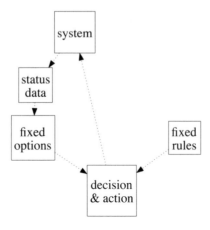

Figure 3.3   The general information flow of the data learning model

scientific theories these have been somehow proven through experiments. And being mental models, theories are updated – or even replaced – from time to time, in 'scientific revolutions'.

The concept of mental models goes back to antiquity – for instance in the 'ideas' of Socrates, as abstract and content-rich 'images' of reality. The term 'mental models' was coined by Scottish psychologist Kenneth Craik in the 1940s (Senge et al., 1994, p.237), about the same time when related advances were made in psychology regarding 'brainstorming' (Osborn, 1953). Mental models have two interpretations: (a) the semi-permanent tacit maps of the world which people hold in their long term memory; (b) the short term perceptions which people build up as part of their everyday reasoning process. It is possible that the short-term models accumulate and form (or influence the shaping of) long-term mental models, and in this book we shall use the first type of mental maps, of the more permanent nature.

Let us now take the traffic jam example again and explore the information flows in the 'imprinted' learning model. The system and the specific information (status data) reaching the learning entity are the same. The difference starts at the point of thinking of what to do (options) against traffic jams. The 'imprinted' learning model features a fixed and 'uninformed' mental model, which contains what the learning entity already 'knows' about traffic jams, while this knowledge is not coming from the study of the system of interest. For the sake of argument, let us consider as a mental model the common idea that traffic jams are caused by lack of traffic lanes. This mental model is likely to influence both the options for action and the selection rules for decision. With the 'lack of lanes' mental model, the options for action will be probably turned to the direction of building more roads and expanding the existing ones. Accordingly, the best solutions will be those that are effective in accommodating more vehicles. By adopting these measures, the learning entity expects to reduce a number of traffic jams, which is also a contribution against the global situation (system) – Figure 3.4.

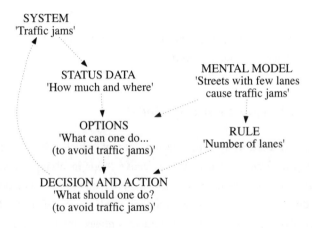

Figure 3.4   Example of the imprinted learning model

In the imprinted learning model, the learning entity is still principally guided by obtaining status data – for instance regarding the frequency and location of traffic jams. The new feature of the mental model provides some guidance to the search of the options and the establishment of the selection rules, but in this case it comes pre-defined – or 'imprinted' in the learning entity's mind – as it has no connection with the system of interest. The general information flow of the imprinted learning model is presented in Figure 3.5.

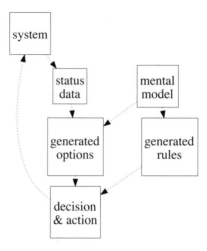

Figure 3.5   The imprinted learning model: the rules are generated from an 'imprinted' mental model

3.2.3   The Deeper Learning Model

We can now proceed to a deeper learning model, which is equivalent to the 'double loop learning' – that is, two effective loops involving the action. In this third information flow model we have a more realistic mental model, which is shaped directly from the system. Although it takes some effort to shape the mental model of the system, the immediate advantages are more realistic learning as well as more autonomy in thinking and acting – that is, escaping the 'automatic' or 'instinctive' action produced respectively in the first two information flow models.

Let us take the traffic jam example once more and explore the information flows in the 'deeper' learning model. The system and status data are the same as in the previous models. In resemblance to the imprinted learning model, the deeper model also contains a mental model, but this one now is derived from the knowledge of the particular system, perhaps complemented with the study of other similar systems – for instance, through the planners' experience or through scientific research. The mental model of the system in this case is 'how traffic jams are generated', and can be expressed, for instance as in Figure

3.6 in a CLD representation.

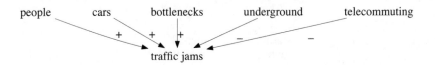

Figure 3.6   A CLD-type mental model of what causes traffic jams

Mental models most likely have no universal validity, and are usually debat-able as not everyone is expected to agree on causal mechanisms, for instance. Nonetheless, their value is in making visible and sharing the way we think, and pointing towards factors of intervention. The selection rules can be effective-ness against the occurrence of traffic jams (in general) or specific indicators – for instance, traffic jam incidents at certain locations and/or hours. Once again, by adopting these measures the learning entity expects to reduce the number of traffic jams, which is also a contribution against the global situation (system).

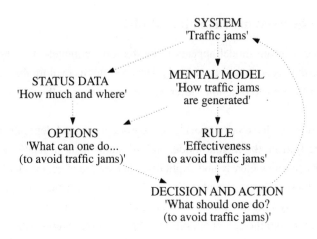

Figure 3.7   Example of the deeper learning model

The deeper learning model transmits and updates information in two ways: the facts (status data) and the mechanism of how these facts are produced (men-tal model) – Figure 3.8.

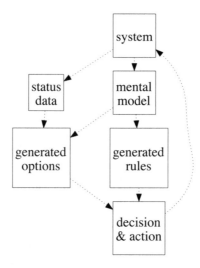

Figure 3.8   The deeper learning model: the mental model is formed 'first hand', by looking to learn how the system works

3.2.4   The Systems Learning Model

The deeper learning model appears to be the most complete and capable of informing the decision maker properly. However, let us explore that model in terms of structure and function – after all, we are learning to think in a 'systems way'.

Up to now we have been conceiving action options and defining selection rules directly from the mental model and the status data. In fact, it would be very handy to know clearly and explicitly what we are after: exactly what we wish to achieve – that is, our objectives. We can make this the first special feature of a new 'systems learning model', in which the objectives guide and focus the search for both the action options and the selection criteria. The objectives are formed from knowledge (status data and mental model) and the collective preferences of the community – the collection of which may be quite challenging.

With the addition of objectives, the new systems learning model features three types of elements, which we identify as X, Y, and Z. The first part relates to the target system, containing the status data and our mental model of the system (Y). The second part contains our objectives (Z), or what we wish to achieve regarding the target system, as well as the selection rules or criteria for decision making, which must be in accordance with the objectives. Finally, the third part relates to the action (X): starting with many possible options and finishing with the committed option, after the selection process of decision making – Figure 3.9.

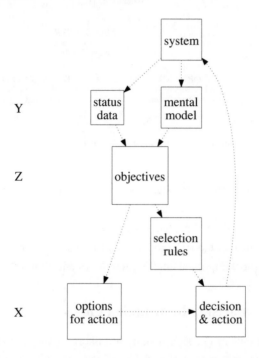

Figure 3.9   The information flow of the systems learning model defines an 'extended mental model' with three parts: X, Y, and Z

Let us see the traffic jam example applied to the systems learning model. In fact this would be the same as the deeper learning model, except here we have the explicit expression of objectives – for instance, to 'avoid traffic jams'. The difference may not seem much, but is as important as knowing something implicitly versus stating that clearly. This is specially appreciated in more complicated cases, as we will begin to see in the case studies of the last chapters.

The systems learning model of information flow defines an extended mental

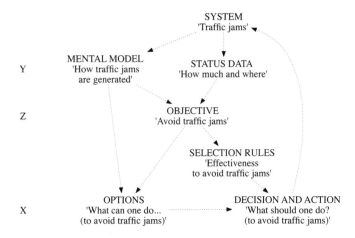

Figure 3.10   Example of the integrated learning model

model, in which planners and stakeholders join the original physical system to become a whole – or an extended system. In comparison, the scientific or empirical knowledge about the target system becomes a 'restricted' mental model. The extended mental model introduced by the systems learning model is conceptually the most important contribution of systems thinking in planning.

3.2.5   Summarising Information Flows

Information flows in decision making are likely to vary among practices. If 'informed' decisions matter, then the more elaborate models are better investments. Mental models are essential features of the more elaborate models, and require significant attention in their construction – including communication with the stakeholders. In particular, the systems learning model, featured in this book, presents an extended mental model constituted by the 'reduced mental model' regarding the system of interest plus the intervention of the planning operation. This extended mental model can still be effective even when used with very reduced mental models of the target system (for instance, to a few parameters, as we will consider in the case study examples by the end of the book), when this becomes necessary, as it still presents a structured and functioning system with three types of elements: X, Y, and Z.

The next section on causal relationships helps to look into the discovery and formation of the restricted or scientific mental models (referring merely to the target or physical system of interest), as well as how to make them explicit so they can be shared, checked, and updated or corrected. Such restricted mental models can take the form of process diagrams (see § 4.1 about concise process diagrams, or CPD) or causal diagrams (see § 2.3.2 about causal loop diagrams, or CLD, and § 4.2 about descriptive causal diagrams, or DCD).

Finally, the last section of this chapter is dedicated to defining problems in a structured 'systems way', following the more elaborate systems learning model, which is an even better investment in informed decision making. In this way, the planning problem is defined as an extended tri-partite mental model including action (X), conditions or concerns (Y) and objectives (Z), formed with the help of descriptive causal diagrams (DCD – § 4.2).

3.3 Causal Relationships

Planners often take interest in indicators and indices (see the Glossary for definitions and distinction) to obtain, store, and communicate information (status data) about their systems of interest. Indicators and indices are usually presented in sets, but they are not necessarily related to each other. In a fashion similar to that of an automobile dashboard, a medical exam, or a control panel of an industrial unit, sets of indicators and indices constitute apparently fragmented mental models – frequently presented in the form of lists. For planners interested in a limited number of items, represented by indicators and/ or indices, then this information may be sufficient – provided it is adequately integrated in an extended mental model.

On the other hand, planners who deal with complete sets of indicators that (intend to) represent the whole system of interest – see, for instance, Esty et al. (2005); EEA (2005); OECD (2003, 1993) – will need to know whether and how these indicators and indices influence each other – or, seen in the other direction, how each one of these depends on others. It becomes clear that in systems approaches, knowing the system elements is not enough: we need to 'connect the points' before we can see the full picture, or the system of interest, and understand how it functions. This brings us to the issue of causality, which is an important step towards systems thinking as it prepares for structured, functional, and explicit mental models – whether 'restricted', such as the physical system of interest, or 'extended', such as the definition of the planning problem.

Causality is the relationship between causes and effects, describing what happens (effect) and the reasons for it happening (cause). Much of the relevant literature refers to cause-and-effect relationships as 'causation', but this best refers to 'the act of causing something' which is not a kind of relationship. Causality refers to the dynamic – from the Greek δύναμις (force) – relationships between entities, in a way that one 'forces' the other behave in a certain way. For instance, heating an object makes its temperature increase (Figure 3.11). The same relationship can be seen from another point of view, for instance from that of the temperature of the object: it increases because the object is being heated.

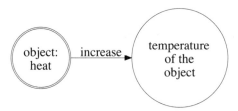

Figure 3.11   Heating an object makes its temperature increase; or else, the temperature of an object increases after heating

As may be expected, not every relationship is causal. Let us consider the action of rolling a dice (Figure 3.12). What is the relationship between the roll and the face value? Unless the dice is specially fabricated, we cannot claim with confidence that the exact occurrence was produced because of the particular style of rolling of the dice. For normal dice, the relationship between the roll and the value of the occurrence is not possible to control nor predict.

In some cases – perhaps in many, depending on the subject – we may not know exactly or clearly whether a relationship is causal or non-causal. Let us consider the geographic distance between Verona and Venice, which is about 105 km (Figure 3.13). The spatial relationship between the two cities – that is how close or how far apart they are located – may be the result of coincidence, for instance because the founders of both cities liked the respective locations,

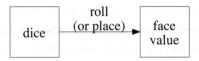

Figure 3.12   *The roll of the dice produces (exposes) but does not determine the face value*

or it could be that the founders of the newer city had the intention to build their own city at approximately 100 km from the older one – for instance, to be reached within a few hours by horse.

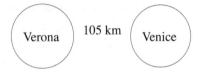

Figure 3.13   *The geographic relationship (for instance, the straight-line distance) between the location of the two cities may or may not be causal*

Thinking of causality enables people to explain observed events by discovering and attributing possible causes – as, for instance, in basic scientific research or in criminal investigation – or to predict effects from the study of actions or events – as, for instance, in impact assessment. Both explanation and prediction have been perennial human quests, but they have not always been approached rationally through causality. For instance, Homer's *Iliad* demonstrates armies with admirable physical and strategic capabilities, but at the same time the army leaders depend on predictions based on prophecies from Apollo.

Causality has been an enduring issue in philosophy, with key figures including Aristotle, David Hume, and Carl Hempel among many. One of the more recent and influential enquiries of causality in explanation was brought to prominence by Hempel and Oppenheim (1948), in the context of science. A more demanding philosophical movement was initiated by Scriven (1959, 1975), arguing that to explain an event is to identify its cause. Even though it

appears desirable to have complete causal explanations, some cases are difficult to understand, particularly when the situations involve grand dimensions,
multiple interactions, and uncertainty – as frequently happens in planning. In
cases of complex systems, where people do not have sufficient information nor
understanding, a typical reaction is over-simplification – for instance using selected indicators or aggregated information in the form of indices as a kind of
'black boxes', ignoring causality altogether.

In most cases it is impossible to prove causality. Causal statements or as-
sertions often remain mere assumptions, as scientific (that is, experimental)
proof may require extraordinary resources (for instance time, money, materials
or energy) and often encounters ethical obstacles (for instance, when involving issues of human welfare). Statistical analysis, although it can infer some
correlations between the observed values of system parameters, is 'blind' to
causality and constitutes no proof even when it asserts no correlation – as is
the case with time delays between events, for instance. The next best substitute to proving causality is probably trying to understand 'how things work',
as well as documenting and sharing knowledge, beliefs, and assumptions about
causality. It is highly important to document and express the 'causal maps' that
are often kept in people's minds. Thus, in this book we formalise the mental
models through a special type of causal diagrams, adapted for planning – the
descriptive causal diagrams (DCD) in Chapter 4.

Being a key feature of dynamic mental models, causality and its clear communication is argued to be a key issue in planning. This argument is made
more strongly in this book than it has been in the previous systems thinking
approaches to planning, for instance by McLoughlin and Chadwick. In the
background, new legal obligations created by impact assessment – for instance
environmental impact assessment (EIA), strategic environmental assessment
(SEA), appropriate assessment (AA) – are ready to welcome expository mental models in the name of transparency.

3.3.1 Deductive or Scientific Approach

The scientific community is chiefly concerned with proofs, giving great importance to the examination rather than the construction of hypotheses. The
same applies to causality statements: they are treated as hypotheses, and are

subject to examination. While the scientific method allows great freedom regarding the formulation of hypotheses, the limiting factor is the proof: testing a hypothesis (or its inverse, 'null hypothesis') typically by experiment. If a hypothesis passes this testing phase through a rigorous procedure, it is elevated to a 'theory' status, having the value of a *bona fide* rule out of which we can trustfully extract useful deduced information.This sets the background for the deductive approach to causality, in which a hypothesis about a causal relationship is formed, tested, and then proven or rejected – much like in the classic scientific method – Figure 3.14.

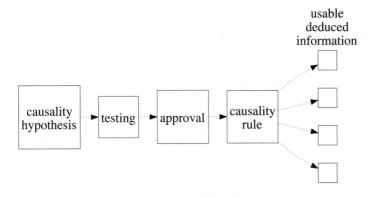

Figure 3.14   The deductive approach to causality is concerned with the proof rather than the formulation of the causality rule

This type of thinking about causality sets out to determine experimentally or semi-experimentally (for instance, with statistical analysis) causal relationships – for instance, that certain effects are present when certain presumed causes are also present. As the trust in this thinking is placed in the testing phase, many 'black box' (that is, non-causal) hypotheses may find their way to being tested – and even proven, if the figures so indicate. In the case of a hypothesis such as 'unemployment subsidy hinders employment search', for instance, which involves humans and any experiment may raise questions of ethics, the causal relationship may be examined or tested with the help of statistics – that is, using observed data about the effect of interest, having occurred in known situations, where the causes are suspected to be included, as if an experiment had been carried out. However 'scientific' this type of thinking may be, it does not determine anything about causality – that is, the causal mechanism expressed in the hypothesis. In reality, it only examines correlation or co-variance between phenomena.

The deductive approach is well accepted in the scientific community as it follows the scientific method, and also it is handy to use with numerical techniques such as statistics analyses. Its shortcomings are likely to arise from the reduced attention to the formulation of the hypotheses regarding causality – in particular regarding the causal mechanisms (often substituted by input-output models), as well as the excessive security bestowed in the scientific proof.

3.3.2 Inductive or Investigative Approach

In the inductive approach, the focus is different. Data are collected after observations and a causal relationship is induced – that is, a generalised conclusion is inferred from particular instances. This type of thinking draws on theory and/or experience to describe the mechanism by which the effect is thought to be caused. As a process it is less formal than the scientific method, and its main concern is the formulation rather than the proof of the causal hypothesis.

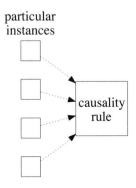

Figure 3.15 *The inductive approach to causality is concerned with the careful formulation of causal hypotheses, rather than proving their validity*

While science typically examines hypotheses, the formulation of these hypotheses remains an unexplored terrain. The inductive approach is interested precisely in this unexplored terrain. Formulating a hypothesis – about causality or any other relation – involves a number of capacities: observation, interpretation, pattern recognition, references (knowledge), information processing, to name but a few. Thus, the formulation of hypotheses has many alternative approaches, which makes it very similar to creative processes – for example in the arts domain. The inductive approach takes interest in the explicit causal relationships, drawing on theory and/ or experience to describe the mechanisms by which the effects are thought to be caused. As such, it does not stand any chance of being characterised as 'scientific' by the current scientific paradigm, and produces tentative, yet complete explanations behind the hypotheses.

Advantages of the inductive approach include an invitation to thinking: creative, critical, informed, rational. As such, the inductive approach is more receptive to less formal information, such as knowledge that cannot be or has not been proven. The greatest disadvantage of the inductive approach is that the causal relationships are not proven – although they can be conceived wisely and realistically, and can even be debated – so in terms of scientific merit they may be credited no more than mere assumptions or non-tested hypotheses.

With its interest in explicit mental models rather than seeking proofs, this book turns to the inductive approach, which is chiefly concerned with the construction of plausible causal mechanisms. Indeed, these often remain mere assumptions, but their practical value is not in the kudos given by a 'proof status'. Rather, the value of the causal mechanisms is in seeing them, sharing them, thinking about them, discussing them, and making them as realistic as possible – even if they are technically no more than assumptions on paper or on the computer screen.

3.3.3   Heuristics

In practical applications, people use various techniques to discover, verify, and attribute causality. These techniques are often called 'heuristics', from the Greek ευρίσκειν (to find). Heuristics employ one or more general rules, which can be inductive or deductive. Some common heuristics are explained below, and then summarised in Table 3.1.

A basic premise of causality is that the effect must follow the cause (in time) – and not vice versa. This is the 'precedence' heuristic rule. For instance: Homer got soaked in the rain, and the next day he was ill (Figure 3.16). Thus, we exclude the cause-and-effect direction going from ill to soaked on the grounds of temporal appearance.

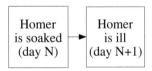

Figure 3.16   The precedence heuristic examines the order of appearance of events

Cause and effect events usually occur next to each other, in time and/ or space. This premise constitutes the 'proximity' heuristic rule. For instance, the current unemployment rate is due to this government's policies (Figure 3.17). This, as the following three deductive heuristics, are based on mental models – for instance, could we be observing the effects of the previous government's policies? Thus, the implementation of the heuristic is subject to the appropriateness and correctness of the mental model to be used for each particular case.

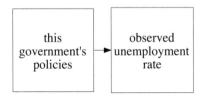

Figure 3.17   The proximity heuristic examines time (or space) patterns between events

Cause and effect sometimes share common aspects or are observed within the same theme. This premise establishes the 'similarity' heuristic – for instance, my son has abdominal pains; he must have eaten something bad (Figure 3.18). The integrity and appropriateness of the mental model is crucial to the correct implementation of the heuristic. For instance, why should we make an exclusive association of abdominal pains with food ingestion? After all, there are other organs in the abdomen that could be causing the pain.

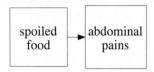

Figure 3.18   The similarity heuristic seeks causality between effects within the same theme

Cause and effect events often have similar (numerical) patterns. This premise establishes the heuristic of 'covariation'. For instance, many people have had accidents at this stretch of the road; my accident must have been caused by the particularity (conditions) of the road (Figure 3.19). Once more, the integrity and appropriateness of the mental model is crucial to the correct implementation of the heuristic. For instance, why should my accident have been caused by the same reasons as all (or most of) the others? There may have been common parameters to include and associate, such as fog formation and the geometry of the road, but my accident may have been simply due to carelessness or tiredness.

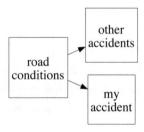

Figure 3.19   The covariation heuristic relates data patterns

There is another basic premise of causality, namely that certain conditions must exist for an effect to appear. This establishes the 'sine qua non' – in Latin, literally: '(cause) without which not' – heuristic rule. It seeks necessary conditions for causality, but gives no guarantee that these are also sufficient conditions. For instance, he was a saver, so he made a fortune (Figure 3.20). We can consider this as an inductive heuristic since it seeks to establish causal mechanisms, although it excludes the sufficiency term. This heuristic is useful for the formulation of causal hypotheses (for instance, producing mental models such as the one we saw in Figure 3.6), but not for the formulation of complete, dependable causal statements, because it does not provide a thorough examination.

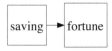

Figure 3.20   The 'sine qua non' heuristic seeks necessary conditions

Finally, the heuristic of 'mechanisms' applies knowledge (or belief) about underlying causal mechanisms to establish causality. As such, this heuristic takes an inductive approach to construct the rule for the particular case, invites critical thinking, requires the explicit expression of mental models, and recruits all knowledge and understanding of 'how things work'. We shall consider many examples of this heuristic in the last chapters of this book.

3.3.4   Semantics

Semantics is concerned with meaning – from Greek σημαίνειν (to signify). Many researchers – for instance from the system dynamics and systems thinking schools – are strongly in favour of directed graphs to understand and represent causality, showing clear preference over the alternatives of mathematical equations, isolated parameters such as indicators, or informal descriptions such as text.

To claim that we know the minimum about causality, we must consider, link, and understand (a) who and what is involved, (b) the action, or who does what, (c) the cause-and-effect relationships, and (d) the effects themselves – see also Perdicoúlis and Glasson (2007); Perdicoúlis (2008a). These four semantic categories are summarised in Table 3.2.

System elements indicate who and what is involved. These can be ecosystem components (for example humans, forest, atmosphere), actors (for example construction teams, operation teams), or new developments (for example

Table 3.1   Common causality heuristics

Heuristics	Approach	Premise and Comments
Precedence	Deductive	The effect must follow the cause (in time) and not vice versa.
Proximity	Deductive	Cause and effect usually have temporal and/ or spatial proximity. Depends on mental models.
Similarity	Deductive	Cause and effect usually share common aspects; similar patterns are known from other cases. Depends on mental models.
Covariation	Deductive	Cause and effect have similar (numerical) patterns. Depends on mental models.
'Sine Qua Non'	Inductive	Certain conditions are necessary for an effect to appear; this does not ensure a sufficient condition for causality.
Mechanisms	Inductive	Underlying causal mechanisms must be expressed. Invites critical thinking. Requires knowledge and understanding.

motorways, power plants). The action is usually expressed by the main 'action verbs' (for example build, operate) and explicitly or implicitly associated to the actors. Cause-and-effect relationships reveal how the proposed action will cause certain changes. In text, for instance, this can be expressed by special verbs (for example to cause). Effect is what happens to a system element because of an action or the change in another system element. Effects can be, for instance, an increase or decrease in magnitude (for example of noise, of biodiversity).

These semantic categories can be expressed in a variety of media such as text, matrices, or diagrams, but require special attention for clarity and precision. Most of these media are capable of presenting the appropriate level of aggregation of information for communicating causality, and permit alterna-

Table 3.2   Semantic categories of causality

Semantic Category	Meaning	Examples
System Elements	Who and what is involved	Investor, local residents, land, motorway, power plant
Action	The proposed action of the plan, usually expressed by the main 'action verbs'	To build, to operate
Cause-and-Effect Relationship	The pathway through which the action will cause changes	To cause
Effect	Changes in system elements	Decrease in noise, decrease in biodiversity

tive or concurrent 'zoom in' and 'zoom out' versions – that is, less and more aggregated views, respectively. This book features a special type of diagrams for the communication of this information, presented in § 4.2.

The analysis of causality semantics is qualitative. Perhaps the first and most common approach is to carry it out mentally. This mental operation is informal, so everyone is allowed to think in any way they wish. The difficulty here is perhaps how to keep in memory all the information in each semantic category. It is the same challenge as taking apart a machine and then remembering all the pieces and how they were put together. Certain types of memory (for example what is known as 'photographic memory') and experience (that is, having done this several times) are considerable advantages. On the other hand, a large amount of information poses an additional challenge to an analyst's memory, and perhaps to the communication of this information to other people.

When starting by text, the analysis of causality semantics can be carried out with the help of manual marking, as indicated in Table 3.3 and illustrated in § 7.1.

Text mark-up is a good help for causality analysis, starting with the tran-

Table 3.3   Sample options for marking up text manually

Semantic Category	Text	Example	Markup
Element	quantifiable noun	population, satisfaction	SMALL CAPS
Action	verb & specifier	install, create policy	**boldface**
Causality	verb	causes, provokes	sans serif
Effect	quantifiable noun	increase, decrease	*italics*

scription of the text into diagrams, where errors, uncertainties, and omissions are likely to be encountered. Once in a diagrammatic form, the analysis should easily seek (a) the links between elements, (b) omissions such as elements, effects, or links, (c) errors such as writing 'increase' instead of 'decrease', (d) certain pathways of interest (for example, from action to outcomes), (e) significant side-effects, and many more aspects depending on the specific requirements of the analysts.

Instead of manual marking, the analysis of causality semantics can be carried out with the help of specialised software for qualitative data analysis (QDA). Table 3.4 presents a selection of QDA software.

Table 3.4   A selection of qualitative data analysis (QDA) software

Software	URL
Atlas/ti	http://www.atlasti.com/
NVivo	http://www.qsrinternational.com/
TAMS Analyzer	http://tamsys.sourceforge.net/
HyperRESEARCH	http://www.researchware.com/

3.4   Problem Setup

Having considered the best information flow model for a more 'informed' decision (§ 3.2), and having appreciated the importance of mental models with explicit causal explanations (§ 3.3), in this section we build a special way to define and solve planning problems. The novelty in this approach is that problems are defined as three-part questions in a system. The people who define the question have the liberty and the responsibility to discover the system – with its elements and their interactions – in which to set up the problem.

Mathematics, the par excellence field of problems, teaches us that problems are to be solved – not to give worries – and how we can organise our thought to set them up and solve them. Problem – from the Greek πρόβλημα – means 'thrown forward' (from πρό, forward + βάλλειν, to throw, as in 'ballistics') and refers to a question. The original idea about 'problems' was that if someone threw a question forward, then someone might answer it. Formal problem-solving has been led by mathematics for centuries, assisted by science – the Latin version of the Greek επιστήμη and its wealth of accumulated knowledge, including problem-solving methods. Problem-solving in 'non-scientific' contexts sometimes allows for innovative and creative solutions, and we will see this in the case studies, by the end of the book.

Everything related to problems is frequently subsumed into a main concern: to solve them. Problem perception, definition, and analysis are thus considered as part of problem-solving. At times, even implementation of a solution to a problem may be considered as part of a problem-solving duty – many people do appreciate 'action' as opposed to 'theorizing'. So, 'problem-solving' wraps many functions under its heading which, once ordered, may form a general problem-solving protocol such as Figure 3.21.

The problem solving protocol of Figure 3.21 is highly abstract and merely indicative. We all have different ways – or methods – of solving problems: how we perceive them, analyse them, identify solutions, choose the best solution, etc. Nobody says that we all have to do it the same way, and not even that one person must solve the same problem always in the same manner. Problem-solving is creative, therefore it brings satisfaction – simply, it's fun! Although we cannot expect absolute uniformity in problem-solving, it is possible to identify patterns, which allows the compilation of methods.

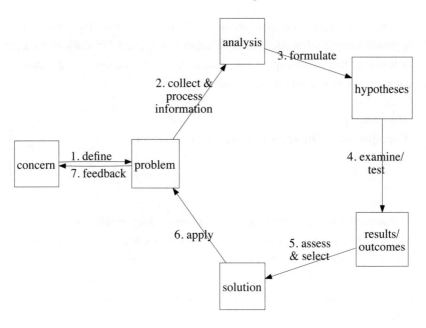

Figure 3.21   A generic sequential protocol of problem solving; this version contains six stages and seven actions

Mathematics teaches us that well-structured problems have three parts: conditions (Y), objectives (Z), and action (X). For mathematicians, problems are simply requests for 'doing X in conditions Y to obtain result Z'. This holds true for as simple problems as '$x + 2 = 5$', up to admittedly complex non-mathematical problems such as 'what can we do (X) to reduce poverty (Z) on Earth (Y)'. Let us recall a classic math problem from the first grade of elementary school (Example 3.1), and discover its 'XYZ' underlying structure.

Example 3.1   The apple problem in an XYZ form

Johnny has five apples (Y). How many apples must mom give (X) to Johnny if he needs to end up with ten apples (Z)?

Many problems are set up in this manner, whether we are solving for X, Y, or

Z – except it is up to us to discover their underlying structure. The same 'apple problem' can be formulated as an equation (Example 3.2), which is a more common mathematical expression – although very abstract, so its components could be referring to anything, not just apples.

Example 3.2   The apple problem as an equation

$5 + x = 10$

The earlier systems thinking contributions of McLoughlin and Chadwick had a preference for mathematical expressions such as objective functions, which are suitable when the interests are quantitative. In this book we shall consider problems in qualitative terms, which is a more suitable approach to handle problems that revolve around questions of action, such as 'what should we do?'.

Giving special attention to action perhaps indicates a shift towards 'strategic planning' (Napier et al., 1998; Bryson, 1995; Goodstein et al., 1993), although previous attempts to what has been called 'strategic spatial planning' have been somewhat vague and quite remote from systems thinking (Sartorio, 2005). In this book we keep the focus on systems in spatial planning, and action is the key notion for managing, running, or controlling the systems – to satisfy McLoughlin's idea about system control. For instance, a simple spatial problem (or question) for the urban planner could be something along the lines of Example 3.3.

Example 3.3   Spatial question ('problem') for the urban planner

Where (location) should we trace the road from A to B (condition 1) so that it remains below 200km in length (condition 2)?

The problem of Example 3.3 takes another form in this book to adapt to systems thinking – for instance, as in Example 3.4.

Example 3.4   Strategic problem for the system planner

What should we do (X) to get people (or goods etc.) from A to B (Z) in less than two hours (Y)?

In this 'strategic' transformation of the problem the question is about action, so the answer may not be just a series of points in space – that is, the answer may not be a road. For instance, if what we intend to be transporting mostly is people, we may come up with an alternative technological solution such as 'telecommunications'. If the answer must be indeed a road, then we can proceed with a mapping exercise or GIS query.

Let us now consider the three options for defining an 'XYZ' problem, according to what is known and what we need to solve for. Solving for X, we are either conceiving (in a creative mode) or forecasting (in a predictive mode) an action – Figure 3.22. For instance, a question we could be asking to conceive action is 'What should we do? [in order to ...]', and this is very common in policy making. The predictive mode for action is not very common – for instance, 'What will agent 'A' do? [given that ...]' could be encountered in a 'games' approach to planning – for instance, between stakeholders. It is the first of these two cases that we shall be examining in this book.

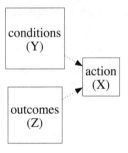

Figure 3.22   Information flow in solving for the action; in this book we use the creative mode, not the predictive mode

Solving for Y, we are either discovering (in an exploratory mode) or designing (in a normative mode) a set of conditions or a system that we are interested in – Figure 3.23. The configuration of Figure 3.23 is favourable to considering the system Y as an input–output transformer, whether in an exploratory or a normative mode: 'if we did X and obtained Z, then Y is of this or that type'. This is not in the spirit of systems thinking, thus this particular problem setting is not used in this book.

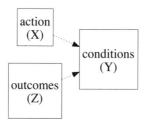

Figure 3.23   *Information flow in solving for the system; in this book we use neither the exploratory nor the normative mode*

Solving for Z, we are determining an outcome either as a forecast (in a predictive mode) or as objectives (in a normative mode) – Figure 3.24. For instance, questions we may want to ask when defining objectives, which will later on serve as normative references, are of the type 'What do we want to achieve? When? Where?'. On the other hand, in a predictive mode – for instance, in a simulation of an action – we may be interested in knowing 'What is likely to happen? Where? When?' In this book we use both forecasting (in simulations) and normative modes (when defining the objectives), but we do not explicitly define the problem as in Figure 3.24.

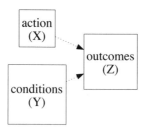

Figure 3.24   *Information flow in solving for the objectives (normative mode) or outcomes (predictive mode)*

Table 3.5 provides a summary, relating the XYZ parts of the problem to tasks such as conception, forecasting, or design, modes such as creative, predictive, or normative, and operations such as policy making or physical planning.

Table 3.5   Solving for X, Y, or Z

Part	Time	Task	Mode	Use	Here
X	future	conceive	creative	policy making	Yes
X	future	forecast	predictive	speculation	No
Y	past	explain	exploratory	science/ knowledge	No
Y	future	design	creative	engineering	No
Z	future	define objectives	normative	planning	Yes
Z	future	forecast	predictive	ex ante assessment	Yes

The answers to some problem configurations are more complicated than others. For instance, when we are asking to explain a system (Figure 3.23), the answer must be a complete description of a system, in structural and functional terms, which in principle contains much information – for example a weather system or an ecosystem – and thus may be challenging to describe and communicate. As a counter-example, when we are asking to identify the action (Figure 3.22) likely to produce a certain outcome in a given system, the answer can be as simple as 'do nothing', which is very easy to describe and communicate.

The XYZ model leaves much liberty to apply the XYZ notions. What is a condition or concern (Y) and what is an objective (Z), or even the action (X), can be defined with more, less, or just the right amount of information. As we will see in several examples in the case studies, it is possible to adjust this information by tiering, which provides a type of 'zoom in' and/ or 'zoom out' exercises – increasing or reducing the detail of the information we consider (or 'see') in each tier.

Various aspects of the planning problem can be defined tentatively, and adjusted in subsequent iterations. For instance, we can define the scope of the information in an initial attempt, and then adjust the scale of the information to come closer to what is most interesting or appropriate for the particular case. Although we will consider a number of examples that illustrate the art of 'problem definition', every case is unique and it takes practice to perfect the art. It is up to the modeller and the support team to define the problem right – or rather, conveniently and appropriately.

In the planning problems considered in this book, the unknown is action (X) and we must know quite well what we intend to achieve, or the objectives (Z), as well as the specific conditions of the system that raise concerns (Y). For example, the generic form of the problem is: 'Which action (X) will satisfy the objectives (Z) in a given set of conditions (Y)?' This action is expected to produce the intended outcomes (Z'), but it is likely to also produce unexpected outcomes (Z'') – both of which shall modify the original conditions of concern (Y) – Figure 3.25.

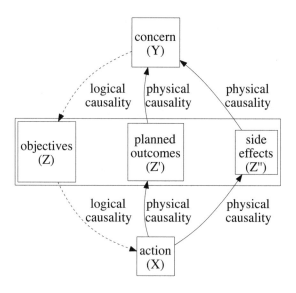

Figure 3.25   The XYZ problem formulation seen as a process – that is, the effects are presented as a 'stage' (square)

In the case studies presented in the last chapters of the book we will see that a variety of problem setups are possible, each one with its own special implications. In fact, each case study in this book closes with a review of the type of the definition of the problem. Figure 3.25 presents a generic model of the definition of the planning problem, including the solution (the action X in the context of this book) and its implications. Let us make three important observations at this point, with the help of Figure 3.25.

The first observation is that the three 'Z' elements are grouped together in a rectangle because they are all 'outcomes' of different types: objectives (Z) that we intend to achieve with our action, actual outcomes that were planned (Z'), and actual outcomes that were not planned but occurred – that is, the side-effects or impacts (Z''). The planned outcomes (Z') should be as close to the objectives (Z) as possible, otherwise we have a 'gap'. In fact, these two should be a kind of mirror image of each other: the objectives (Z) before the action and the planned outcomes (Z') after the action takes place. The planned outcomes (Z') can be also used as criteria for our decision, to select the best or more appropriate action among a set of alternatives.

The second observation on Figure 3.25 is that there are two kinds of causality arrows. The dashed arrows (- - - - - ➤) represent 'logical causality', which are mental operations such as interpretations or inferences – for instance, 'what is required to achieve this objective', or 'what this concern means'. The solid arrows (———➤) represent 'physical causality', which will be manifested in the physical system. Both these types of causality information are important for the expression of our mental models, in terms of assumptions (mostly regarding the logical causality) and of knowledge (mostly regarding the physical causality).

The third observation relates Figure 3.25 with the PSR and DPSIR models we considered earlier (Figures 2.8 and 2.9 respectively). The XYZ model can be seen as a variation of the PSR and the DPSIR models (§ 2.3.6). Figure 3.26 presents the DPSIR model in a rather unusual way: the base is a simplified version of the PSR model, which is very similar to the XYZ model. Contrary to the original representation of the DPSIR model (Figure 2.9), two of its elements (D and I) are being represented as interactions among the PSR elements.

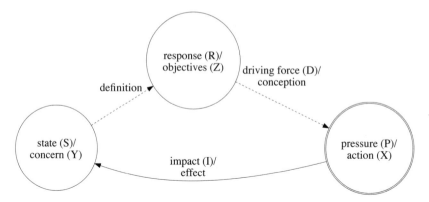

Figure 3.26   The DPSIR model in relation to the XYZ alternative

3.5   Conclusion

In this chapter we considered several information flows related to decision making, the most complete of which require a considerable investment in constructing explicit mental models about the system of interest. The most realistic mental models include causal relationships, so we need to be familiar with causality heuristics and expressions. We also considered that one of the most complete definitions of the planning problem includes an 'extended mental model' in an XYZ form, organised and expressed through the mental model of the target system plus the intervention. This way, even if we take a limited look at the target system, first we become conscious of that (and expand our information scope, if necessary), and then we always have an explicitly considered system in which we participate, reason, plan, decide, and act. In the following chapter we shall consider two special diagramming techniques prepared to assist the expression and processing of information.

4. Diagramming Techniques

Technical text, such as that found in plans or projects, often expresses the stages of a process and – optionally – the operations involved. Process diagrams are suitable to transcribe such expressions from text to an appropriate diagrammatic form, so the sequence of the process becomes easier to follow, understand, and verify. We can do this in a simple and effective way with concise process diagrams (CPD). There is an inherent shortcoming of process diagrams, though: the effects of each operation or action are typically incorporated in the stage following the action, so they are not always (or easily) expressed clearly.

Due to this shortcoming, and although they are useful as an interface with technical text, process diagrams are not suitable for the study of cause and effect relationships. This is where we need an appropriate type of causal diagram such as descriptive causal diagrams (DCD), which are designed to express and communicate cause and effect relationships in a way that is suitable for planning – in particular, to accommodate each one of the four semantics categories of causality (§ 3.3): the system elements, the action, the effects, and the causal links.

From the perspective of the user, the practical difference between process and causal diagrams is about the effects, which are expressed on the causality arrows in the causal diagrams (DCD); depending on our interest, the effects in process diagrams (CPD) are sometimes blended together with the state of the system elements, in which way they may in some cases disappear from our view and consideration, while in others they are expressed individually as 'stages' (squares).

4.1   Concise Process Diagrams

Process diagrams are encountered in a variety of application contexts, from algorithm architecture to petroleum refinery plans. While most process diagrams involve elaborate technical drawings, in this book we use the simplified, custom-made concise process diagrams (CPD). We have already used such diagrams in previous chapters of this book, such as the learning models (Figures 3.3 to 3.9). In this section we learn about the conventions of the CPDs, which are compatible with the other type of diagrams used in this book: the descriptive causal diagrams (DCD, § 4.2, and CLD, § 2.3.2).

Process is a sequence of operations and stages, with a beginning and an end. As common examples we know recipes, algorithms, driving instructions, etc. Process diagrams contain: (a) nodes, which represent key stages of the process (for example ingredients, recognisable phases); (b) arrows, or directed edges, which represent operations (for example action and technical details). The conventions of the concise process diagrams (CPD) are summarised in Table 4.1.

Table 4.1   Summary of the conventions for the representation of concise process diagrams (CPD)

Semantic Category	Text	Example	Graphic
Stage	noun; identifiable state	decision, data	stage
Operation	verb or noun	produce (v.); production (n.)	action →
To next stage (certain)			⟶
To next stage (uncertain)			- - - - ➤
Information flow			·······➤

The generic form of a process diagram is presented in Figure 4.1.

A stage is an identifiable step in the process. We can have as many or as few stages as deemed necessary for a particular purpose. Operation is the action that transforms one stage to the next. This is typically transmitted with a verb or noun. The continuity between stages of the process is represented with arrows, on which we can mark the operation and other details – for instance, processing time. CPDs distinguish three types of arrows: solid (⟶) when the link is expressed with certainty, dashed (- - - - ➤) when we are not sure about

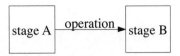

Figure 4.1   Generic process diagram; here we see the 'stages', not the 'changes' caused by each operation – cf. Figure 4.6

that path (descriptive or normative), and dotted (·······►) for the generic case of transmission of information – Figures 4.2 and 4.3.

Figure 4.2   An explicit way to express the flow of information from one stage to the next

However, since we are not contributing to significant knowledge with the operation 'transmission', which indicates the flow of information, in CPDs we can simplify all these cases with the special type of dotted arrow (·······►), which concisely indicates the transmission of information (Figure 4.3).

Figure 4.3   A concise way to express the flow of information from one stage to the next

Process diagrams may serve both descriptive and normative functions. Figure 4.4, for instance, describes the process of forming a project proposal and applying for planning permission, in the conventions of the concise process diagram (CPD).

The dashed arrows (- - - - - ►) at the final stages of the process indicate the uncertainty about the final outcome, which can be an approval or a rejection

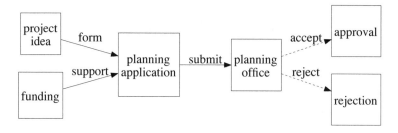

Figure 4.4   Example of a process in the CPD conventions

– that is, one of two possible pathways.

4.2   Descriptive Causal Diagrams

This section describes the rules for how to draw Descriptive Causal Diagrams (DCD). The conventions are organised by the four semantics categories of causality (Table 3.2), explained in the text below, summarised in Table 4.2, and illustrated in Figures 4.6 and 4.7.

System elements are quantifiable nouns (for example population, satisfaction). Sometimes these have a physical presence, such as 'residents of village Q', while other times they are abstract parameters of the system, such as 'flood level'. Even though we cannot always guarantee – and in most Descriptive Causal Diagram (DCD) applications we do not need – a numerical value for system elements, they must be at least in principle quantifiable. Sometimes it is not easy, or it is even impossible to measure a system element (for example the 'image' of an institution), but it is possible that one or more people have an idea about its numerical value and are capable of making a quantitative estimate.

System elements could be represented graphically as shapes such as circles, rectangles, or ellipses, which can be coloured or not. In case of using colour, it is a good idea to keep a simple palette – for example from two to four colours. System elements could be grouped or clustered so they appear at the same hierarchical level – for example all actions (X) in the same row. The convention for this book is to represent all elements of descriptive causal diagrams (DCD) as circles of different types (Figure 4.5), avoiding the use of colour.

Table 4.2   Summary of the conventions for DCDs

Semantic Category	Text	Example	Graphic
Element	quantifiable noun	population, satisfaction	generic system element
Action	verb and specifier	install, create	action
Causality (physical)	verb	causes, provokes	⎯⎯⎯►
Causality (logical)	verb; logical term	means, requires; therefore	- - - - ►
Effect	quantifiable noun	increase, enhancement*	effect ►

Action is expressed with a verb (for example install, build). Sometimes a specifier or a brief explanation is necessary, for instance regarding the element where the action takes place. Action in DCDs is marked as text within the shape of the system element that originates it, separated from the system element by a colon (:) and starting on a new line. Action is labelled as 'X', and various actions are identified by numbers – for example X1, X2, etc. An action can be explained or specified in more detail at a next level, identified by a lower-case letter – for example X1a, X1b, etc. If a third level of detail is necessary, then that is numbered by a lower-case roman numeral in parentheses – for example X1a(i), X1a(ii), etc. These conventions are not universal, but they must be consistent within each case.

We consider two types of cause-and-effect relationships: (a) a physical causality, which is expressed in text with a verb (for example causes, provokes) and in a graphical form as a solid arrow (for example ⎯⎯⎯► ; (b) a logical causality, expressed in text also as a verb (for example means, requires) or as a logical term (for example therefore), and in a graphical form as a dashed arrow (- - - - ►). In either of the cause-and-effect relationships, causality

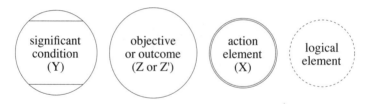

Figure 4.5   Causal diagrams have four kinds of elements

arrows are uni-directional. If two elements have a two-way, or bi-directional relationship, this requires two separate arrows. In this book we use a third type of arrows, the dotted arrows (·······►), but these are not causal and are not part of the DCD conventions. Dotted arrows signify 'information flow' in a generic form, in process diagrams (CPD), for instance when we join information from Y and Z to seek solution X (Figure 3.22).

The effects or changes caused to a system element by an action (or passive changes) from another system element are expressed in text as quantifiable nouns, and we distinguish two types: (a) objective, factual, or measurable effects (for example increase, decrease), and (b) subjective changes, or value judgements (for example improvement*, enhancement*). The effects that involve value judgements are marked with an asterisk (*) on the right side of the effect. The point of view of these judgements must be shared by many, and be unquestionable – for instance, not disputed by groups of conflicting interests.

Effects are marked on the (solid-line) arrow of the physical causality. The dashed arrows, which represent logical causality, carry not effects but the logical predicates that we associate between two system elements (for example Y 'implies' Z). The descriptive, absolute, or definite effects are a feature of the descriptive causal diagrams (DCD). This contrasts with the relative effects (for example same or '+', in the fashion of systems thinking and/or system dynamics), which may be sufficient (or perhaps even preferable) for study purposes or numerical simulation. Planners often need to think 'concretely' and 'pragmatically', so they wish to know at a glance – that is, without having to make mental processing – what the effect of a causal relationship is thought to be.

Figure 4.6 illustrates a generic descriptive causal diagram that in text would be expressed (or can be 'read') as:

'The action at the upstream element has an effect to the down-stream element.'

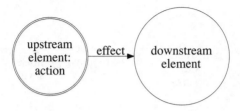

Figure 4.6   Generic DCD; contrary to process diagrams, in DCDs we can clearly see the effects caused by the action

In this case the causality is transmitted by a non-specialised word – that is 'has'. More obvious verbs would be 'causes', 'produces', 'brings about', etc. The effect must be stated succinctly and unambiguously: for example increase, decrease.

Let us consider a simple specific example. In a housing context, Figure 4.7 expresses graphically as a DCD a statement of our knowledge or assumption such as:

'Upgrading the safety of a house increases its reselling price.'

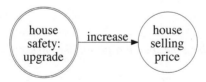

Figure 4.7   An example of a DCD

Now that we have seen the basic expression of DCDs, let us make two ob-servations about the description of time and space in causal diagrams. The dimension of time is important to action and to effects (for instance, when a delay is expected). Therefore, when necessary, time can be marked together with action and/or effects, or marked otherwise – for instance, in the case of sequential action (Figure 6.9). Figure 4.8 shows an example of marking the duration of the effect of an action in a causal diagram, as a characteristic of the effect.

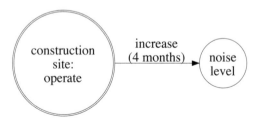

Figure 4.8   Describing the duration of the effect of a localised action

Descriptive causal diagrams are not the best medium for describing space, although they are very good in describing action and effects. As action often has spatial dimensions, we can refer to spatial information in DCDs in relation to actions and/ or effects, as necessary. Figure 4.9 shows an example of marking spatial information regarding the effect of a permanent action, pointing to a geographic map for further details.

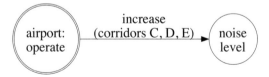

Figure 4.9   Describing the spatial aspect of the effects of a permanent action

4.3   Diagramming Software

Process and causal diagrams (CPD and DCD) can be hand-drawn using pencil and paper. However, computer software could make editing easier – for instance, when moving elements or renaming causal relationships. Of the various kinds of software that could potentially draw process or causal diagrams, bitmap software (like photographic or painting applications) provide no more editing facilities than hand-drawing. Specialised diagramming software can facilitate drawing and editing, and even arrange the layout for visualising and/ or studying alternative perspectives – for instance, placing all action proposals in a row, or displaying tiers hierarchically. Table 4.3 presents a selection of diagramming software.

Table 4.3   A selection of diagramming software

Software	URL
GraphViz	`http://www.graphviz.org/`
OpenOffice Draw	`http://www.openoffice.org/` `product/draw.html`
OmniGraffle	`http://www.omnigroup.com/` `products/OmniGraffle/`

OmniGraffle and *OpenOffice.org Draw* provide easy graphical editing, which may produce fast results. *GraphViz* requires manual editing of the code, as illustrated in Example 4.1, and in most cases the layout arrangement is optimised automatically – yet with some options for author intervention. *OmniGraffle* also allows automatic layout in some cases, based on the *GraphViz* engine.

Example 4.1   The *GraphViz* code for Figure 4.7

```
digraph D {
//NODES
A [shape=doublecircle,label='house
safety:\nupgrade'];
B [shape=circle,label='house\nselling price'];
//EDGES
A -> B [label='increase'];
//STOP
}
```

Using appropriate software to draw process and causal diagrams can facilitate the operation, and produce diagrams that are well organised and easy to read. In this book we use small diagrams, due to space limitations of the page size. Larger diagrams can accommodate more information, and can still be ordered and re-ordered in a variety of ways – as indicated in the smaller diagrams of the case studies, in the last chapters of the book. Eventually, large causal diagrams can have a role similar to that of technical drawings or geographic maps, namely present specialised information in an efficient and appropriate medium.

4.4   Conclusion

In this chapter we took a technical look at the conventions of two types of specialised diagrams: descriptive causal diagrams (DCD), which are essential in the graphical expression of the definition of the planning problem in an 'XYZ' form, and concise process diagrams (CPD), which are often useful as a direct interface to technical text. Both of these will be applied in the next chapters, to process the case study material.

5. New Plans

This chapter is dedicated to new planning initiatives, as opposed to the revision of existing plans that follow in the next two chapters. The first section of the chapter refers to the method for defining and solving the planning problem in a systems approach, as we saw in § 3.4. The following sections present applications of the method in a selection of case studies, starting with easy and accessible examples.

5.1 Planning Method

In this section we will establish the method for planning in a systems way, based on the definition and solution of the planning problem in an XYZ form, as we saw in Chapter 3. To give an identification to this method, we can call it 'explicative causal thinking' (ECT) as it features more explanations than other planning methods, insisting specifically on causal relationships. ECT is an alternative to other planning methods such as the Soft Systems Methodology (SSM) or the Strategic Choice Approach (SCA) that we saw in Chapter 2. What makes ECT different, and justifies its name, is the type of diagrams it requires – namely the descriptive causal diagrams (DCD) we saw in Chapter 4 – as well as its guidelines, summarised in Table 5.1 and detailed in the text below.

Many system modellers share a common conviction that comes from experience, summarised in the principle: 'do not start drawing systems without a purpose'. This purpose is many times expressed in the definition of a problem. Thus, when we attempt to represent the system of our planning interest in the form of a model, with elements and interactions, we must do that after defining the problem – preferably in an XYZ formulation. There is one exception, though, and that is when modelling, in a 'draft' mode, helps people to explore the target systems and discover the issues of concern.

In most types of engineering and classic architecture, the construction follows the design, or the plan. There are two notable exceptions, environmental

Table 5.1   The guidelines of the ECT planning method

Guideline	Summary
Problem Modelling	With the exception of an exploratory function, modelling of the extended system follows the definition of the problem.
Reverse Blueprints	Mental models of the structure and function of the 'restricted' system can be expressed as CLD 'reverse blueprints' or processes (CPD).
System Scoping	In both the restricted system and the problem model, the information is selected by appropriate scoping.
Transversal Systems	Thematic sectioning is discouraged, and systems must be defined by relevance to the defined problem.
Full Causality	Besides the physical causality, in the extended system (problem) we must also consider logical causality.
Information Sources	The sources of information involve scientific knowledge as well as the stakeholders' empirical knowledge, reasoning, will, and assumptions.

engineering and landscape architecture, where the object – namely, Nature – precedes the design. Whereas mechanical or electrical engineering and classic architecture prepare their drawings in what has been termed as 'blueprints', there are rarely any blueprints for the systems that a planner is interested in. This 'rarely' refers to the built environment where one can find a record of the design with which these systems were built, but still rarely with all the intended detail such as social interactions. In this sense, the planner can produce the 'reverse blueprints' of the target system, thus clarifying and formalising their mental model, for instance with the help of causal loop diagrams (CLD, § 2.3.2) or concise process diagrams (CPD, § 4.1).

In planning we must always select what is relevant and important for our particular effort – that is, we cannot make provisions for everything, everywhere, and forever. This selection of the information that is relevant can be achieved through a scoping exercise, and this should be done with great care and attention. We may have to return to our scoping exercise after having made some progress, in order to refine the scope by including or excluding information.

Some specialists may restrict the scoping exercise to the object of their speciality (and/or interest), in which case they are likely to define 'the system' by thematic sectioning (for example by transport planning, geology, or climatology) or geographic sectioning – for example the national territory or a river basin. It is more 'natural' to make scoping by structural and functional considerations – for example the local community – especially with the definition of the problem as a guide for relevance.

Systems contain not only elements, but also relationships among these elements. As we cannot consider that 'everything relates to everything', we are called to consider only the most important and relevant relationships between system elements. Besides the physical cause and effect relationships – for instance, from an action to its effect(s) – we also consider logical relationships that reveal our reasoning (for example defining objectives, thinking of action options) and make it explicit and easy to understand, verify, and share.

Information about the system has several sources: it can be our knowledge, which can be scientific (because we or others have discovered that through experimentation) or empirical (because we have first hand experience); it can be our assumptions or beliefs, which sometimes serve to complement or even substitute knowledge; or it can be our will to achieve or to do something in the system. Good planning shares all that information, which is particularly important if it comes from different people and points of view.

The ECT planning process for new problems involves six stages, as illustrated in Figure 5.1 and described in the list below.

1. *Case Study* – This provides an overview of the case, with the purpose to focus our interest and thoughts; some exploratory modelling may be handy at this stage; more information about the case study may be provided in subsequent stages, as long as the focus of interest is not com-

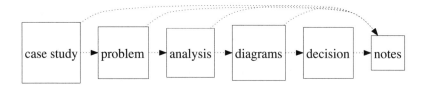

Figure 5.1   Overview of the ECT planning process for new problems

promised.

2. *Problem* – Using the focus and information from the case study, we can formalise the problem in an XYZ form, preferably as a simple question (that is, in several lines of text) seeking for the action that will satisfy the defined objectives.

3. *Analysis* – Having formalised the definition of the problem, we may seek further information than that provided in the presentation of the case study; here we may start exploring possible solutions.

4. *Diagrams* – To help keep track of the information involved in the formal problem definition, the analysis, and problem solving, we can organise this information in descriptive causal diagrams (DCD).

5. *Decision Making* – To make a decision, we must know the options for action and the selection criteria; with criteria the expected outcomes of the action (corresponding to the objectives), we can review the proposed solutions in the diagrams and select the best option of proposed action.

6. *Notes* – After each stage, as well as at the end of the application, we record any deviations from the standard methodology, any difficulties that may have arisen, implications of the solutions, and any other observations (for instance, about the problem type) that may help to refine the planning operation for now, and the planning method in the future.

5.2 Example: Home Safety

This first example explains and illustrates only key stages of the process of planning with ECT, employing a very simple case study. Some of the diagrams considered here are the 'insider's view' (that is, they are not to be shown as final versions), and are presented for explanation only.

5.2.1 Exploration

We may start to plan with either clear or vague ideas about what is involved, what we want to achieve, etc. In the first case, we can skip the exploration stage and go straight to the definition of the problem. The exploration stage is optional, geared towards those with a vague idea about the planning problem, and is an invitation to explore, think, and discover who and what is involved, what each system element means, how system elements link, etc.

Let us illustrate with a case study where the concern is home safety. We can start modelling in an exploratory mode, and thus create a system element called 'home safety' and present it as our 'main concern' with the conventions of DCDs (Figure 5.2). From there we can start exploring what home safety means. For the sake of simplicity, let us suppose that home safety means (or is about) fire protection and break-in protection. Again after the DCD conventions, we mark these new elements and their relations to our main concern.

Then we proceed to explore (or to think) a little further: what is necessary to have fire protection and break-in protection? From experience or from professional advice we gather that fire protection requires fire extinguishers (supposing we do not consider the more expensive option of a built-in system) and break-in protection relies mostly on safety doors and windows. This thinking makes us consider what we might be doing next: install these safety devices. At this point we may conclude our exploration stage because we have reached some resolutions regarding our concern. So far we have a semi-structured problem, so the next step will be to formalise our exploration into an XYZ type of problem.

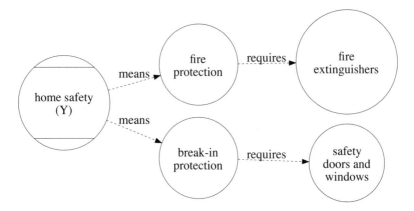

Figure 5.2   Initial exploratory (un-structured) diagram; without using many labels yet, here we can express our main concern (identified by the two horizontal lines, above and below the text), analyse what this means, and then creatively explore what is required

5.2.2   Problem

After the exploration stage, or starting to plan with previous experience, we can formulate the problem in XYZ terms. For the case of home safety, considered above, we can configure the problem as in Example 5.1.

Example 5.1   The home safety problem

What can we do (X) to increase home safety (Y) in the sense of fire and break-in protection (Z)?

When formulating the problem to assign Xs, Ys, and Zs, we have the opportunity to add more system elements and discover functional relationships among system elements that were not present in the first simple diagram. In the problem diagram we have the opportunity to mark two other types of 'Z' elements (that is, relevant to the objectives): the outcomes (Z') that we do expect to occur as a result of our action, and those that are not expected to occur – which are a type of 'side effects' (Z'').

5.2.3 Diagram

Figure 5.3 illustrates the problem configuration for the home safety case. The diagram contains more information than the succinct expression of the problem, much of which was revealed through thinking and creative exploration – for example the objectives (Z1 and Z2) and the respective solutions (X1 and X2).

The problem diagram contains the definition of the problem, the solutions, and the follow-up from action to outcomes. At this point it is a good idea to verify whether our scope is complete and adequate, whether our marked relationships make sense and are correct, whether we are missing something important, and generally assess the information presented.

5.2.4 Qualitative Simulation

Although we have already simulated our solutions in the problem diagram (Figure 5.3), we may wish to see our solution and its outcomes in isolation. This can be done for the purpose of assessing the effectiveness of our solutions, and is especially useful in complex diagrams. Thus, a simulation-only diagram can be obtained by hiding the objectives (Z) and their relationships from view, since their function was to transfer us from the situation of concern (Y) to the right action (X). This may not be necessary for more experienced modellers, but let us present it in this introductory illustration.

Figure 5.4 presents the simulation diagram for the home safety example. Although we added nothing new comparing to the problem diagram, we do see the results of the action more clearly: its outcomes and the pathway to improving the situation (Y) of our concern.

ECT is conceived to function with qualitative information, so the simulation is also qualitative – as opposed, for instance, to numerical simulation. This qualitative information must be followed by hand – thus it can be called 'manual' – from the beginning to the end. In Figure 5.4, for instance, we have two beginnings and three ends. All (or most) pathways must be satisfactory (for example if insurance expenses had increased, that would not be satisfactory), otherwise we must go back to the problem stage and seek alterations to the solutions, objectives, etc. or seek mitigation measures.

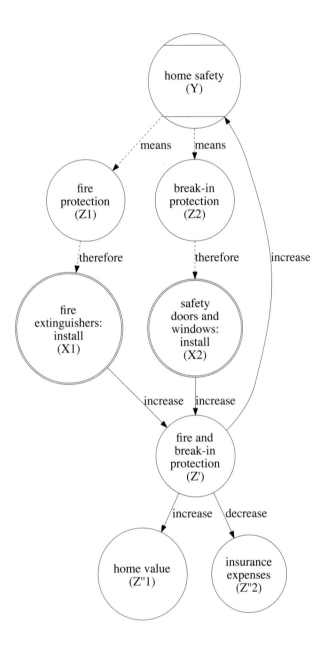

Figure 5.3   ECT: problem configuration diagram (XYZ structure)

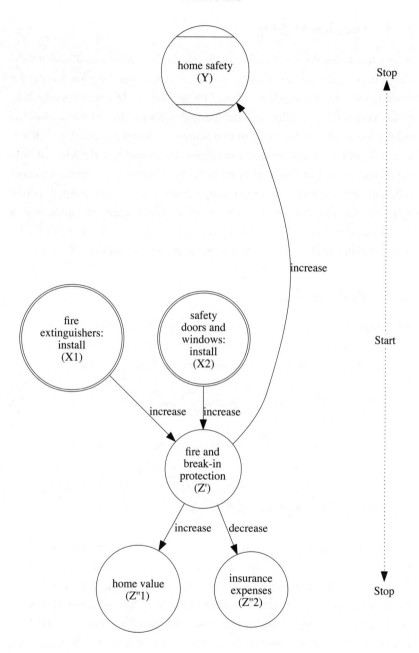

Figure 5.4   ECT: qualitative (or 'manual') simulation diagram

5.2.5   Decision Making

After considering the solutions we proposed for the problem, and having simulated these solutions, we must now reach a conclusion. In other words, we
must decide what the single solution of the problem is. In a very concise definition, decision means choosing and fixing that choice. If we have considered
only one solution (such as a set of two actions, as in this example), the choice
is between that solution or doing nothing – for instance, if the forecast outcomes appear very undesirable. If we have considered two or more alternative
solutions, the decision involves choosing the best one, and that is usually done
by laying out selection criteria, as we will see in subsequent examples. In this
case, since the solution is the only option and its outcomes are acceptable, the
decision is favourable – that is, to accept the proposed solution.

5.2.6   Problem Type

As a final observation, let us consider the type of the problem in this introductory illustration. We can obtain this information from the problem diagram
(Figure 5.3) and create a 'type diagram' – Figure 5.5.

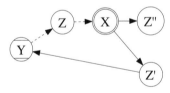

Figure 5.5   Type of the home safety problem

The interpretation of the problem type diagram has a methodological interest, and also serves to verify the 'robustness' of the solution. For instance,
Figure 5.5 demonstrates that the initial concern (Y) is reached by a first order outcome (Z′), which can be considered as a 'robust' solution. If Y were
reached after a second or higher order outcome, then the solution would have
been less robust (or more vulnerable), subject to a number of influences to the
intermediate outcomes – or, simply, more things could interfere or 'go wrong'.
In general, our forecasting certainty and functional confidence about the chain

of outcomes satisfying the concerns tends to be reduced in proportion to its length – whether in a linear or non-linear fashion. In addition to the robustness issue, the side effects in this case have been considered as beneficial and as such they reinforce the appropriateness of the proposed solution.

5.3   Example: Personal Protection

This second example is built around a single diagram, and is the first full application of the ECT planning method. Since the application of the full planning method may appear difficult for the first time, let us consider a simple case study at the personal domain – placed at the lower end of the 'well-being' scale – to which readers may relate both as planners and as stakeholders. In this case we shall identify alternative solutions to the problem, and shall exercise our decision making skills regarding the selection criteria.

5.3.1   Case Study

Dehydration of a living organism is a health hazard, so it easily becomes the prime concern of an informed person when visiting very hot and arid environments, where water evaporates fast, or extremely cold places where water easily takes the form of ice. Let us take the case of sunbathing on a beach, which tends to be a popular activity in the ever-increasing global culture.

Some people like to sunbathe in order to get a sun tan for aesthetic reasons, while others for health reasons – for example to activate provitamin D as prevention of rickets. Despite the sun protection lotions against UV radiation, sun bathers often risk dehydration – that is, excessive water loss from their body.

5.3.2   Problem

With the introductory information of the case study, let us formulate the problem (Example 5.2). The condition of concern regarding our system (the human body) is dehydration, which we can call 'Y'. In fact, since we insist on maintaining the sunbathing activity, the body will be naturally dehydrating on the hot beach. Therefore, our objective (Z) is to rehydrate the body, to compensate for the water that is being continuously lost. So, what should we do (X)?

Example 5.2   The sunbathing problem

When dehydrated from sunbathing on a hot beach (Y), what can one do (X) to re-hydrate (Z)?

5.3.3   Analysis

At this point let us explore what we know and how we think, so this analysis is about mental models. In a rather naive approach, we could seek our solutions 'by imitation', from observing what people usually do (apparently to re-hydrate) on the beach: for instance, some drink water, others drink fizzy drinks (soda pops), and others eat ice cream. In a more scientific approach, we can seek some more understanding about hydration: hydration means obtaining isotonic solutions (Figure 5.6) – in other words, containing essential salts and minerals (also known as electrolytes) in the same concentration as in the body, for the purpose of replacing those lost (together with the water) as a result of sweating.

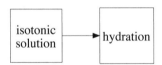

Figure 5.6   The mental model of hydration as a process

We know that plain water does not provide sufficient salts and minerals, so we will rule out this solution – even though many people seem to be adopting it. If we lose water and electrolytes by sweat, let us try to replace these exactly where they are being lost: on the skin. Thus, as a first solution, let us propose spraying the body at intervals with an isotonic solution (X1). As a second solution, let us replenish the lost liquids from the inside: drink some isotonic drink at intervals (X2). And then let us try the 'fun' solutions – after all, the beach is meant to be a fun place: eat some juicy fruit (X3), some ice cream (X4), and drink some soda pop (X5).

Now, let us consider the consequences. Are all these solutions likely to work equally well? Drinking and spraying isotonic water (X1 and X2) should re-hydrate the body, and no side effects are expected – assuming the individual is healthy, and is not exaggerating in the intake quantities. Fruit, ice cream and soda pops (X3, X4, and X5) contain sugar, so sugar intake becomes an issue, whether for concerns of diabetes or energy intake, which means the sunbather could fast accumulate fat. Besides, ice cream is likely not to hydrate at all, as its water content is very low – except for popsicles, but the original solution of ice cream referred to a dairy product. Finally, many soda pops (X5) contain caffeine, which is a diuretic and will have an effect contrary to what we are trying to achieve (Z).

In the way this problem was set up, which reflects the intention of the person to keep on sunbathing, we cannot consider the rather radical solution to stop dehydration by leaving the beach. Namely, the 'Y' element of the problem set dehydration in its context, on the beach, and this cannot be disregarded unless the problem is defined differently.

5.3.4 Diagram

Having analysed and solved the problem, we now can gather all this infor-mation into a global diagram. Figure 5.7 contains the issue of concern (Y), the objective (Z), the various solutions (X1 to X5), and the likely outcomes of each one of these solutions.

The layout of the diagram facilitates the organisation of information. Namely, the activity of interest is at the top, followed by the issue of interest (Y), and then by the objective (Z). The five action proposals are aligned in the next level, followed by the first level of outcomes. Of these outcomes, only Z' is the expected outcome, while $Z1''$ and $Z2''$ were not expected. Finally, we have one more level of outcomes, with $Z2'''$ as a secondary effect, or a second order outcome.

5.3.5 Decision Making

The first and more obvious decision, long before the definition of the problem, was to stay on the hot beach to suntan. The problem was formulated only upon realising that there is a risk of dehydration (Example 5.2). So, even in a rela-tively uncomplicated case study like this, decision making involves more than

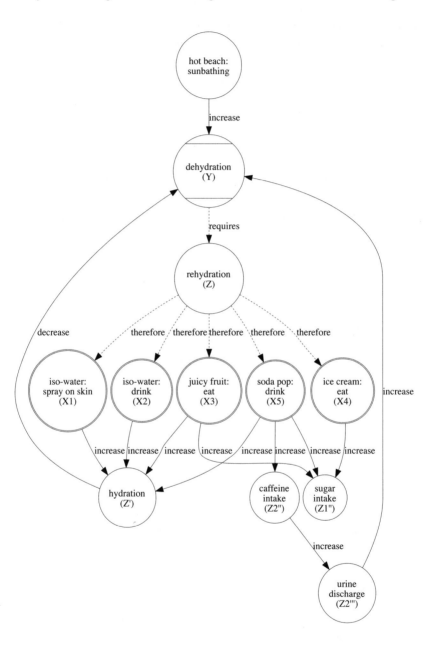

Figure 5.7   The personal protection plan

one event that we call 'decision'. This easy case illustrates at least one possible way of reasoning to select the best solution for our problem.

It is worth noting that before reaching the final and formal decision making of the planning problem, we have already made some 'minor' decisions. For instance, in the analysis – and then in the diagram – we thought that dairy ice cream does not hydrate sufficiently, and so we did not make the causal connection from X4 (ice cream: eat) to Z' (hydration). Our judgement about the hydration capacity of dairy ice cream was probably based on our empirical knowledge about food or the nutritional information on the wrapping, but it may have required some scientific research, which would have delayed the analysis somewhat more. In case we have mis-judged at this stage of the 'minor' or intermediate (as opposed to the final) decision, we would be 'unjustly' excluding a solution to the problem.

To proceed to the final decision, which will allow us to select the best solution for our problem, we must set criteria: standards by which we can make our decision – or where to 'draw the line'. In this case, the definition of the problem allows us to define a single criterion for the final decision making, but through two alternative options: examine the capacity of the solution to either (a) combat dehydration (Y), or (b) to produce a hydration outcome (Z'). In case there are side effects (or second order outcomes), as we have in this case $Z2'''$, these most likely will not impact on the outcomes (for instance hydration: Z'), but on the issues of concern (Y). Thus, the better option to define the decision making criterion is the first one – namely, to test the capacity of the solution (X) to combat dehydration (Y). As a general rule, we always look at our concern (Y) and ensure that it gets satisfied by the solution (X) through the outcomes (Z').

As we saw in § 3.4, the most important outcomes (Z') are mirror images of the objectives (Z) – Figure 3.25. There are a number of other criteria that we have not formally considered. Of these, we have informally considered in our analysis the case of sugar intake, which is crucial for people with dietary restrictions – for instance diabetics. As our subject has been assumed to be 'healthy', this criterion has not been included in the definition of the problem. Another criterion that has not been considered at all is the monetary cost of the solution. If this were a concern, it would have to be included in the definition of the problem, as well.

Now we can initiate the elimination process of the decision making. Examining each solution individually, we find that only solutions X1, X2, X3, and X5 manage to produce hydration – thus we reject option X4. However, we notice that X5 manages to hydrate, but also has a side effect that counter balances its original contribution – therefore we also reject solution X5. Of the remaining three solutions, X3 involves sugar intake, which is unnecessary for the stated purpose in this case, so X3 can be considered as a secondary choice – and only if some sugar intake is deemed necessary. Solutions X1 and X2 appear to be effective, so they can be approved. Since the two chosen solutions are not competitive, they can be implemented either alternatively or jointly – as deemed more appropriate by the user.

5.3.6 Notes

The contribution of systems thinking in this case was to understand in an explicit and 'open' way how to combat dehydration effectively. The thinking described here is probably what many people use but, unless documented, it is never shared. The value of explicative causal thinking (ECT) is in the exposition of the reasoning, which serves to verify one's own reasoning (and correct mistakes, if necessary), and also to share this reasoning with others. For instance, Figure 5.7 presents the obvious and rational thought that 'dehydration requires rehydration'. This is a special type of causal reasoning, of the 'because–then' form, so we mark this causal relationship with a dashed arrow. Although this is an obvious thought, it is not the only way to reason. For instance, one might think (and argue) that 'dehydration requires getting away from the sun' which may stop dehydration, but will not automatically lead to re-hydration. Whether one way of reasoning or another, ECT helps to demonstrate how the person (or the team) thinks, and will not by itself favour one way of thinking or another.

The type of the problem of Example 5.2 (Figure 5.8) has some interesting interactions. Starting with the conditions that represent our main concern (Y), we set objectives (Z), and then explore which actions (X) are suitable to satisfy these objectives. Some actions (X) manage to produce outcomes (Z$'$) which correspond to the original objective (Z), while other solutions (X) have some direct side effects (Z$''$) which are irrelevant to the problem and were not expected, as well as some second order side effects (Z''') which in fact harm the issue of concern (Y).

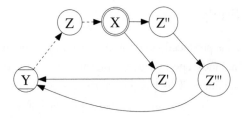

Figure 5.8   The type of the personal protection plan

From conditions to objectives (Y to Z) and from objectives to action (Z to X) we have one type of causal thinking or reasoning ('because–then', or logical causality, expressed with dashed arrows), which in most cases stays as a mental model but in the ECT is explained clearly. The other type of causal thinking, physical causality, is more 'evidential' – that is, easily perceived and/ or measured: from action to outcomes (X to Z', Z'', and Z''') and from outcomes to concerns (Z' to Y).

A final note on the 'gap'. What we define as an objective, and mark as 'Z', is expected to be satisfied by the action (X). In other words, the outcome Z' of the action needs to be the same as – or as close as possible to – the original objective Z. This is the reason we use the same symbol 'Z' for both, with the exception of the 'prime'. In fact, all outcomes of the action are marked as 'Z', and the number of primes increases with the order of the outcomes – that is, as one outcome causes another. This marking has no absolute or universal value, but must be internally clear and consistent for each application.

5.4   Example: Regional Development

In this section we consider a case example of producing a strategic plan, featuring a high-level diagram in which the action is not detailed enough to be directly implementable – we can say that it is 'generic' action, guidelines for action, or 'policy'. Besides solving a planning problem, this example presents a new task: how to 'drill down' in a high-tier action to produce a lower-tier action.

5.4.1   Case Study

The RUR region has produced wine for many centuries, involving a very characteristic 'cultural landscape': terraced vineyards, maintained by people without the use of machinery. This has proven to be a good management practice against the erosion of the soil, and it is also appreciated as cultural heritage intertwined with the lifestyle of the people of the region – at least until our times. UNESCO has recognised the RUR region and listed it in the world heritage list.

In more recent years, mechanisation of the vineyards has brought about a relatively new fashion that creates vineyards along the contour of the hills, with relatively high inclination and without terracing. This is favourable to mechanised farming, which is faster and cheaper than manual labour, but generates unemployment and soil erosion. What future, then, for the RUR region? How can the regional authorities develop RUR? Let us set up a problem.

5.4.2   Problem

From the above description of the case study, we register that the new type of vineyard practice is beginning to shape the conditions in the region. Specifically, this causes three main concerns: an imminent threat to lose its UNESCO status (Y1), a threat to lose soil due to erosion (Y2), and a threat to lose local population (Y3) due to unemployment.

What could the regional community wish to achieve, with the organisational help of the regional authorities? Since the threats come from the new type of vineyard practice, the regional community may wish to 'step back' to its traditional form of being: first keep its landscape terracing (Z1) as part of the physical identity of the region, and then re-establish the traditional activity of wine production methods (Z2), which go hand-in-hand with the traditional vineyard practice – especially in what concerns the annual grape production and processing quantities.

According to the above reasoning, and with the stated assumptions, the problem can be defined as in Example 5.3.

Example 5.3   The RUR problem (original definition)

What can the regional authorities do (X) to safeguard landscape terracing (Z1) and traditional wine production (Z2) if they need to maintain their UNESCO status (Y1), contain soil erosion (Y2), and retain the regional population (Y3)?

In formalising the problem, we have transformed the threats into the concerns of the problem – that is, the 'Y' part. Besides being more positive thinking, this reflects the conditions within which we have set our objectives (the 'Z' elements) – that is, what we wish to achieve. As we noted in the reasoning regarding the formalisation of the problem, the objectives followed from studying the concerns, so the relationship $Y \rightarrow Z$ has been already established.

5.4.3   Analysis

So far we know three conditions of concern in the system, which give us three elements for the system so far: soil, a UNESCO status, and people. We chose to represent these with slightly different names, according to the aspects of our concerns. Thus, soil is represented not by its chemical qualities or average depth, but by 'erosion containment', which we label as Y2. The UNESCO status is represented as such, labelled as Y1, and it has a binary value: either it is attributed or not attributed to the region. Finally, people are grouped together as 'regional population', and labelled as Y3.

Now we must search for what else is included in the system, and register how we think that particular system functions. As we expect our solutions to be part of that system, we can discover the system as we are looking for solutions – that is, actions that are capable of satisfying the objectives we set, or the 'Z' elements. As a start, we reason that to obtain 'landscape terracing' as an objective (Z1), we must terrace all vineyards possible. This defines the action X1. To return to 'traditional wine production' (Z2), we must help all the business people who have the intention to make this change – perhaps regional businesses that wish to convert back to the traditional manufacturing processes. This defines action – or rather policy, as it is merely a guideline, to 'support' – X2.

In thinking of our system and of the solutions to our problem, we find out that we can add a new objective, Z3, which was not defined in the original formulation of the problem. The UNESCO status provides an opportunity (or attraction) for some tourist developments in the region, and the existing population is probably capable of taking advantage of that. Thus, we can add a new 'virtual' element to our system, namely 'tourism potential', which means an opportunity for tourism activity (Z3). This new objective requires a new action, and that is the promotion of tourism in the region (X3).

After this analysis, and since we introduced a new objective, we can redefine the problem for the RUR as in Example 5.4.

Example 5.4   The RUR problem (second definition)

What can the regional authorities do (X) to safeguard landscape terracing (Z1) and traditional wine production (Z2), and stimulate a basic tourism activity (Z3) in the region, if they need to maintain their UNESCO status (Y1), contain soil erosion (Y2), and retain the regional population (Y3)?

5.4.4   Diagrams

We can now start creating a descriptive causal diagram (DCD) to organise the information we have so far. Figure 5.9 presents the RUR plan, which includes what we have considered to be part of the system, the conditions or concerns that we have identified (Y), the objectives (Z) that we defined, and the solutions or actions (X) that we discovered. Drawing such a diagram takes several attempts, and a thorough analysis helps to a great extent, so preparing the diagram is an essential part of the thinking process.

In Figure 5.9, the action elements (from X1 to X3) have been aligned horizontally to provide a focus on the action. For exploration purposes, we could align the objectives or the conditions, to gain different perspectives of the system.

The action proposals of the RUR plan so far (Figure 5.9) have different degrees of 'concreteness'. X1 proposes to terrace vineyards: this is easily implementable, for instance through a project permit system about vineyard develop-

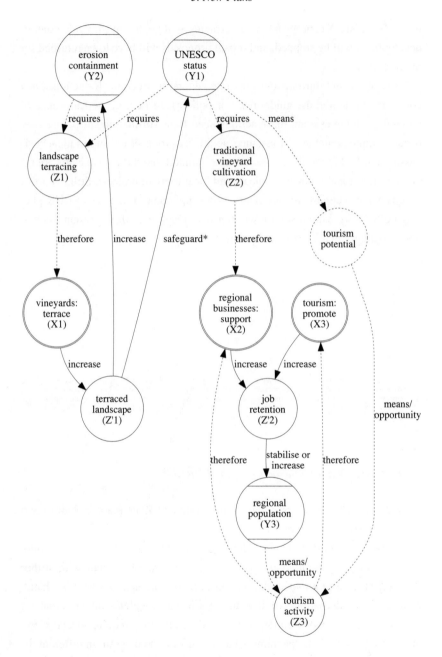

Figure 5.9   The RUR plan; this layout aligns the actions (X1 to X3)

ment. To satisfy X1, proposals with terracing will be approved, while contour development will be stopped, and mixed proposals will have to be returned for modifications.

The second and third actions are quite general instructions for action. They could be considered as 'guidelines', or policies. In fact, in the true sense of a tiered planning system, these actions need to be 'drilled down' before they become implementable. For instance, action X2 proposes to support local businesses, and looking at the figure we are reminded that these businesses are related to traditional vineyard projects and local tourism projects. Still, we must specify what 'support' means. Thus, in a supplement to the above RUR plan (Figure 5.9), we can create a lower tier map (Figure 5.10) to present the two tiers separately in a coordinated manner.

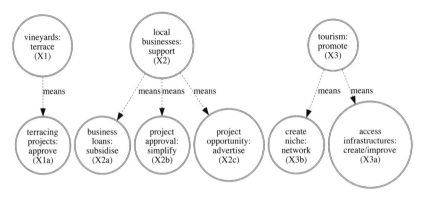

Figure 5.10   Detailing the action of the RUR plan

Alternatively, we can provide a more complete RUR plan, including two tiers of action, as in Figure 5.11.

Although two complementary diagrams may be easier to view and to think about, the single-diagram option permits a global view of the plan, with further advantages regarding its simulation and decision making. On the other hand, adding more information to a diagram – for instance with the intent to make it complete – raises two warnings: (a) large diagrams may require special viewing techniques, such as 'panning' (that is, shifting the diagram in different directions), and may also require special printing techniques, such as 'composite printing' (that is, dividing the diagram into many 'normal' pages) or 'plotting'

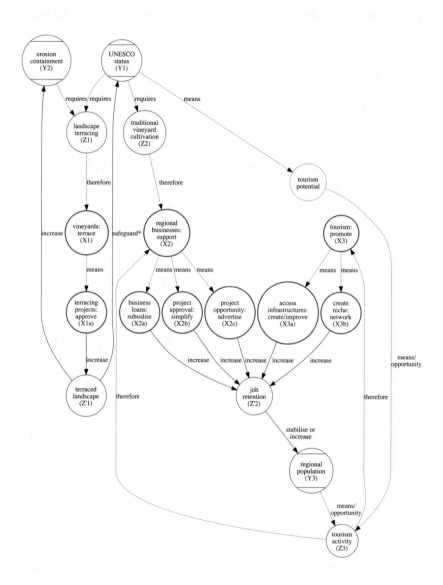

Figure 5.11   The RUR plan with two tiers of action

(that is, using special large-format printers); (b) complex diagrams may require special organisation, for instance keeping all the X elements aligned, or using colour or 'hatching' (that is, line patterns).

5.4.5 Decision Making

So far we have defined the planning problem for RUR, and have come up with some solutions. These solutions in this case are not alternative – that is to say, they are not competing solutions. For each objective we have identified one solution, which can be further divided into more detailed action (Figures 5.10 and 5.11). In such conditions, decision is not a choice among solutions, but a choice between these solutions and no action at all – if, for instance, the action is likely to bring about some ill effects or not produce the expected results. In which case, then, would we approve the plan? What does the decision maker need to know?

In general terms, the decision maker needs to make sure that the proposed action is likely to produce appropriate outcomes (Z'), which are appropriate when they enhance the issues of our concern – expressed as Y. In summary, let us consider as criteria for this decision, then, that the actions (X) shall produce outcomes (Z') that enhance our points of concern (Y). To verify this, we must follow all the pathways of the type $X \rightarrow Z' \rightarrow Y$ and ensure that (a) all effects are correctly marked, and (b) the Y elements do receive an enhancement.

Indeed, by examining the six $X \rightarrow Z' \rightarrow Y$ pathways in Figure 5.11, we verify that all effects are correctly marked and all Y elements receive an enhancement. Therefore, since the contribution of the proposed action is expected to enhance the key aspects of our concern regarding the wine region, the decision regarding the particular RUR plan is favourable.

5.4.6 Notes

The type of the RUR plan includes a new level of elements, the 'Xx' (Figure 5.12). Other than that, the logic of the process is quite simple and robust.

At this point, let us make some more observations. We know that every system – as well as every problem – is defined in the way we find more appropriate for each case. It is true that we may forget system elements or problem

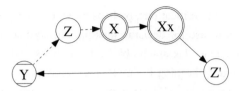

Figure 5.12   The type of the RUR plan

elements, or omit them on purpose, but then we go through a number of iterations that help us catch mistakes and add or subtract elements – for instance,
in the analysis step we had a chance to adjust the definition of our problem.
Of course these iterations cannot be too many, otherwise they would delay our
planning process excessively.

The plan we built for RUR in this section bears some limitations of its system model, and by extension its problem definition. To illustrate that, let us
consider a weakness associated with the 'job retention' ($Z'2$) of Figure 5.11,
which is an outcome of a battery of actions (X2a to X3b). This could in fact
imply the increase of economic activity, and is not studied in sufficient depth.
It is possible that this 'job retention' or economic activity could have some adverse secondary effects (Z'') in aspects which are not included in this system
model. For instance, tourism on a large scale could bring about atypically large
road networks and associated vehicle flows for this region, followed by development patterns in hotels, for instance, that are unusual for the region. Thus,
either (a) the tourism activity objective (Z3) may need to be withdrawn from
the plan proposal on the grounds of these suspicions (and succinct analysis),
or (b) the system model should be enhanced to include the further effects (Z'')
of this 'job retention' or economic activity.

If the problem or the system is deficiently considered, then the decision
made on this basis would also be deficient in its own way. In this particular
case, the decision made in the previous section was based on the simulation of
action proposals, which in turn have been formulated after the definition and
solution of the planning problem. On these grounds, the decision is favourable
to the proposal. If, however, the above mentioned omission in the system were
to have inconvenient consequences, then the decision should not be favourable.
This warning is not issued to obliterate model-based planning, but to raise at-

tention to a number of verifications, perhaps by various people, before reaching a final version to use for decision making. At any rate, by exposing all the reasoning behind the planning problem, its solutions, and the simulation of these solutions, and by keeping it simple, it is possible to capture such mistakes. And any communicated, shared reasoning is always preferable over a non-communicated reasoning, however sovereign the latter might appear.

5.5 Example: Urban Development

In this section we consider an example of producing a development plan for a small city – let us call it URB. The preparation of the plan illustrates an unorthodox practice, when planners prefer to start the process by exploring the system before defining the problem, and thus create a clear mental model of their system with elements and causal links. The risk of proceeding this way is that we may waste time and effort, as exploratory system modelling may digress into irrelevant pathways – and even disorient and discourage the people involved. But we could also be rewarded by doing this as a brainstorming type of exercise, thus discovering important and interesting information.

5.5.1 Case Study

URB is considered a small city of Western Europe, located in rural surroundings but with good access to major urban centres. The population of URB has been growing in the last three decades, which has been mainly due to national immigration and the return of former expatriates. The motive for the national immigration has been associated to a tendency for an urban lifestyle, in search of a 'better life' and abandoning the 'hard' agricultural subsistence lifestyle of generations. The motive for the return of the expatriates is sentimental, and perhaps with a cultural encouragement, the 'love for the fatherland', while it was made possible as living conditions in URB have been improving – most notably with the quality of residential construction and the establishment of regional branches of central government services.

What future, then, for URB? In which direction could the local authority develop URB? What is the 'development problem' to solve? Let us explore the case under the guidance of the master planner of the local authority.

Among the many possibilities to carry out planning at the local level, this case has been elaborated as an example of a three-tier 'bottom-up' model (Figure 5.13).

Figure 5.13   The three-tier 'bottom-up' information model used in the URB planning exercise

The lower of the three tiers is the population or 'general public', including local residents, local special interest groups (for instance, the local association of shop owners), and major stakeholders such as large businesses established in the area. The information flows, in various formal and informal ways, from the lower to the middle tier, which is composed of local officials with special (sectoral) responsibilities such as education, economic affairs, transport, and water resources. Finally, the master planner of the local government receives official information from the second tier, or the local officials, and informal communication from the first tier. Excluding power games and distortion of information, the top-tier master planner is considered well informed and impartial enough to conceive the general development plan of the local government.

The intended URB plan can take one or two forms: namely, it can stay as an orientation (an URB development policy), or it can become a detailed, implementable plan. In this case we present the policy option, which contains orientation for (or general) action. In section 5.4 we saw how to develop a general action into specific, detailed, and implementable action, so we will not be repeating the exercise. This urban development exercise has the value of starting in a different way: namely with the system model.

5.5.2 Exploration

The exploration is an additional step to the planning process established in this chapter, depending on the wish of the people involved in the planning team. The exploration creates a mental model that registers the perceived structure of the system of interest (Figure 5.14). In this case, this mental model 'map' was created after some reflection by the master planner, and was based on thorough knowledge of the system.

We can call Figure 5.14 a 'reverse blueprint', as (a) it resembles a blueprint of a system, similar to those used in the 20th C. in engineering drawings, and (b) it was produced after the system existed, not before – thus, in the reverse direction. This reverse blueprint is descriptive, not normative, and what it presents is mere hypotheses formulated after exposing and amalgamating knowledge about the system. What is important is that it represents the explicit mental model of the planner who is going to propose changes for the development of the system. This blueprint has been 'refined' several times, and can possibly be refined even more. It can also be debated with other planners, the general public, and stakeholders.

The system elements of the reverse blueprint are expressed in quantifiable expressions, some of which are even measurable – for instance, the infrastructure maintenance cost or the public energy consumption. It may be difficult, but it is not totally inaccessible to quantify (even though on arbitrary scales) some notions that are prime concerns to the local government planners, such as 'quality of life', so these also take part in the diagram.

Since the exploration starts with no information about the status of the elements, the links of Figure 5.14 can only be relative. That is, they do not follow the diagramming conventions of the causal diagrams introduced in this book (DCDs, § 4.2), but are created in the fashion of causal loop diagrams (CLDs, § 2.3.2) – except feedback loops are not marked here, since the intent was merely to identify system elements and their causal links. Let us consider, for instance, the following expression from Figure 5.14.

$$\text{quality of life} \xrightarrow{+} \text{immigration} \tag{5.1}$$

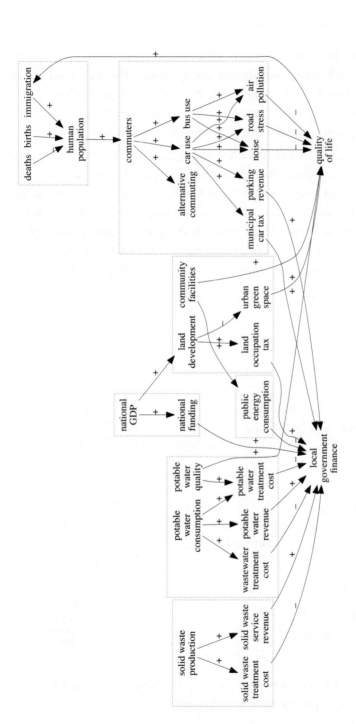

Figure 5.14 The first reverse blueprint of URB: a mental model created from system knowledge, but without a problem focus yet; thematic areas such as water or electricity are marked in dotted boxes

Read from left to right, Equation 5.1 states that a (perceived) higher quality of life will result in more immigration, and a lower quality of life will result in less immigration. Read from right to left, the expression states that immigration depends on the (perceived) quality of life – although in this case we do not know anything about other factors that might also be influencing immigration.

Figure 5.14 was created after a first filtering of what is important in the city. What the master planner learned (or realised) from this exploration exercise and the resulting reverse blueprint was that the system is complex, and that there are three initial concerns: human population, quality of life, and money – that is, national GDP and local government finance. In order to simplify the view of the system, so we can define the core problem, we pass a second filter of selection to identify the concerns of the local government on behalf of the community – Figure 5.15.

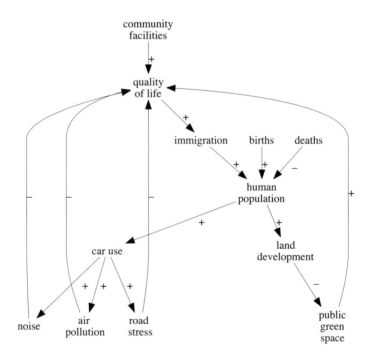

Figure 5.15   The second reverse blueprint of URB: a smaller, more focussed, but still relative causal diagram

5.5.3 Problem

From the system exploration, a number of system parameters could be significant concerns for the local community. These are presented in a second, simpler reverse blueprint: Figure 5.15. Due to the causal links we observe in the second reverse blueprint, the main concern (Y) can be defined as the quality of life of the URB residents. This is affected by five other parameters, which can be defined as the objectives of the problem (Z): community facilities such as schools and health centres for the community should be kept at a good maintenance level; open access public green space in the city (urban parks) and around the city (natural park) should be preserved; and road traffic related nuisances (noise, air pollution, and road stress) should be kept at low levels. As in the previous examples, we shall be looking for the action (X) – 'what to do?' – and thus we can formalise the URB development problem as in Example 5.5.

Example 5.5   The URB development problem

Concerned about the quality of life in URB (Y), what should the city planners do (X) in order to guarantee quiet neighbourhoods (Z1), clean air in the city (Z2), calm streets (Z3), accessible urban and peri-urban public green space (Z4), and community facilities (Z5)?

5.5.4 Analysis

Residential areas can be rendered more quiet if urban traffic is reduced, and this could be achieved by discouraging car use (X1). The specific details for how to discourage car use are not part of the policy, but are left as a tiering exercise. The policy issues only the 'general action', and this is expected to reduce car use (which was the intention), and probably increase the number of urban walking commuters. Two second-order effects of the reduction of urban traffic are expected to make urban streets more 'calm', and residential areas more quiet. These correspond to two of the objectives, Z1 and Z3, which should be satisfied with one action.

Preserving urban and peri-urban public green space probably requires constraining or discouraging 'inwards' and 'outwards' urban sprawl (X2). Besides safeguarding open spaces, this action should also bring about some 'extra' benefits, such as more clear-cut city limits, and good quality urban housing – based on the reasoning that the limited housing will have to be maintained instead of being abandoned in search of new building areas.

Finally, key community facilities such as schools and health centres can be maintained by respective 'updates' of buildings and equipment (X3). Thus, the services to the community are likely to be improved, which contributes to a better quality of life.

5.5.5   Diagram

The formal diagram of the URB policy, as expressed in the problem and including the solutions identified in the analysis, is presented in Figure 5.16. Being a policy, it presents the guidelines for development. All of the proposed action must be worked out in subsequent tiers, until it becomes implementable – which is beyond the scope of this example.

5.5.6   Decision Making

Figure 5.16 presents the main expected outcomes of the proposed action, which are labelled as 'Z'' and 'Z'''. Some of these are the 'mirror images' of the five objectives ('Z'), while others come as side-effects (for instance, Z2b' and Z2a'). The most important verification is that all 'mirror images' of the objectives are satisfied. In addition, all the side-effects are considered to be positive, thus no mitigation is necessary. Thus, the single proposed policy can be approved.

5.5.7   Notes

The policy diagram (Figure 5.16) must be maintained in a good and orderly layout, in order to verify the correspondence between the objectives (Z) and their 'mirror images' – that is, the expected outcomes (Z' and Z''). This particular layout places the concern (Y) and objectives (Z) at the bottom and the action (X) at the top, so the effects (solid lines) 'trickle down' to satisfy the concern (Y).

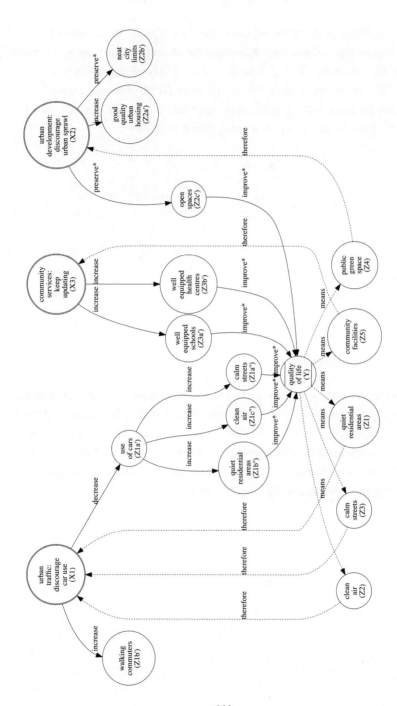

Figure 5.16 The URB development policy; the action at this level of detail serves only as guidance

The typology of the URB policy includes the typical 'Y→Z→X→Z'→Y' loop, plus two special features: (a) some of the desired outcomes are first-order effects (that is, of the 'Z'' type), while others are second-order effects (that is, of the 'Z''' type); (b) some of the second-order effects were not planned for, therefore the proposed action has significant side-effects (Zz'') which, in this case, are positive and therefore no mitigation is necessary.

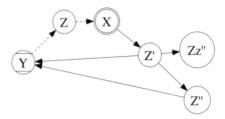

Figure 5.17   The type of the URB policy

5.6   Conclusion

In this chapter we learned how to prepare new plans with the explicative causal thinking (ECT) method, and followed two introductory illustrations and two examples from case studies. Descriptive causal diagrams (DCD) provided the graphic representation of the problem and its solutions, as well as an orientation for decision making. In the next two chapters we shall analyse and consider improvements to already existing plans.

6. Existing Plans

This chapter examines and reconditions existing planning initiatives with the help of an analysis method called 'diagrammatic causal analysis' (DCA) and the descriptive causal diagrams (DCD). Causal analysis of existing plans may be required for a number of reasons, such as the interest of stakeholders to verify the potential for success, or the responsibility of a higher-rank planning authority to verify the coherence of the proposal. One more reason may be legal obligations such as impact assessment – for example strategic environmental assessment (SEA) for the larger-scale, strategic action proposals, or environmental impact assessment (EIA) for investment projects – to which we shall give special attention in the next chapter.

6.1 Analysis Method

In this section we establish the diagrammatic causal analysis (DCA) method, and in the following sections we illustrate the method with case study examples. As a working definition we can consider that DCA transforms any medium of expression – which typically is text – into descriptive causal diagrams (DCD) for the purpose of analysing, verifying, and improving the causal relationships – both physical and logical. The guidelines of the method are explained in the following text and summarised in Table 6.1.

Cause and effect relationships are difficult to keep track of in common technical text. A variety of causal diagrams (for instance CLD – § 2.3.2) are more appropriate, while descriptive causal diagrams (DCD – § 4.2) have been developed specially for the purposes of planning.

It is possible to transform the expression of cause and effect relationships from text to diagram and vice versa. Also, it is possible to transform information from one type of diagram to another – for instance, from concise process diagrams (CPD – § 4.1) to descriptive causal diagrams (DCD – § 4.2) and vice versa. While the information remains the same, its appearance can be different and so we can obtain the desired degree of efficiency for our purposes. The transformation of expressions must be carried out without loss or distortion of information, therefore appropriate techniques and care must be applied.

Table 6.1   The guidelines of the diagrammatic causal analysis (DCA) method

Guideline	Summary
Efficiency of the Medium	Causality is best described, communicated, and verified in causal diagrams.
Transforming Expressions	Expressions of causality can be transformed from text to diagrams and vice versa, as well as from one type of diagrams to another.

The DCA can be applied to the reconditioning of existing plans – that is, action proposals – in a six-stage process, as described in the following list and illustrated in Figure 6.1.

1. *Case Study* – This provides an overview of the case, with the objective to give information of the planning attempt so far (for instance, time frame, spatial scale, problem considered, etc.).

2. *Original Material* – As most plans describe the proposed action in text, this provides the starting point for studying what has been proposed; it is convenient to also include the system conditions and the planning objectives; this text may be a self-contained part of, or the whole plan. When applicable, other types of original material may be considered, such as causal or process diagrams.

3. *First Set of Diagrams* – We start by transcribing the original material directly into a causal diagram (when possible), or first into a process diagram and then into a causal diagram. When diagrams of other types are already provided, these will need to be transformed to causal diagrams.

4. *Observations* – In case the causal diagrams of the original material indicate faults such as missing information, ambiguity, or relationships that do not seem right, we think of appropriate modifications; to respect the

original proposals, we think of corrections only, as opposed to radical changes or re-planning completely.

5. *Second Set of Diagrams* – This takes us one step further, towards a systems view of the problem in an XYZ form, and provides an opportunity for deeper and more appropriate improvements, capable of producing extended solutions to the problem – that is, an improved plan proposal.

6. *Notes* – After each stage, we record any deviations from the standard methodology, any difficulties that may have arisen, implications of the modifications, and any other observations (for instance, about the type of the solutions) that may help to refine the planning modification method in the next application.

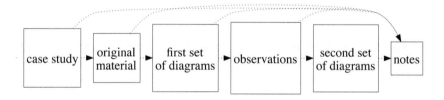

Figure 6.1   Process of the DCA method in reconditioning existing plans

6.2   Example: Health Policy/Strategy

6.2.1   Case Study

The recent sustainable development strategy of a federal authority identifies seven key challenges and corresponding targets, operational objectives, and actions. One of these seven challenges is public health, with a stated overall objective 'to promote good public health on equal conditions and improve protection against health threats'. In this example let us consider one of the guidelines for action, regarding the content of national health policies, which is proposed as self-contained. The exercise of this example can be extended to the rest of the guidelines, regarding public health as well as the other six 'challenges' of the sustainable development strategy.

6.2.2   Original Material

Example 6.1 displays the original text of the federal authority's guideline for action regarding national health policies, of which the selected text is the third of nine items in a list – the only one referring to the responsibility of the national authorities, with the other eight items referring to the responsibilities of the federal authority.

Example 6.1   Health Policy

[National] health policies should aim at creating and implementing strategies to help women and men in achieving and maintaining positive emotional states thus improving their well-being, their subjective perception of quality of life and their physical and mental health.

The selected text raises questions such as 'How is a national health policy to be developed?' 'What should it contain?' and, most importantly, 'What action should the national health policy call for?'

6.2.3   First Set of Diagrams

The text of the recommended action of Example 6.1 represents a process model – as opposed to a causal model – which can be represented diagrammatically as in Figure 6.2.

The process diagram of Figure 6.2 can be transformed into a causal diagram, as in Figure 6.3, after some information processing to fit the formal requirements of the descriptive causal diagrams (DCD).

6.2.4   Observations

The first observation is about terminology. The text is extracted from a sustainable development strategy, and gives guidelines for national health policies. So far, this indicates that (a global) strategy is of a higher rank than (a thematic) policy. Then, within Example 6.1 we are informed that 'policies should create strategies', which establishes that (thematic) strategies are inferior to

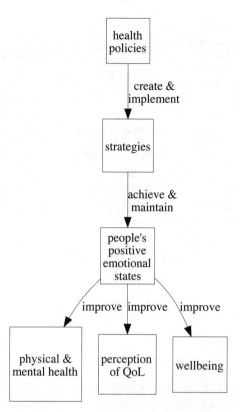

Figure 6.2   Process diagram of the function of health policies

(thematic) policies – Figure 6.4. The repetition of the word strategy, referring to ranks above and below 'policy', may be confusing.

The guidance indicates three main states that are being appreciated as part of the person's health (Y1 to Y3). Surprisingly, the three elements reside strongly in the psychological sphere, with little indication about physical health. This may reflect the federal authority's vision of health, which probably believes in 'mind over body' – although there is no further explanation about the vision of health in the document where the policy is expressed.

The task of every national government within the jurisdiction of the federal authority is to create a national health strategy that will satisfy the unique and general objective of 'positive emotional state'. However, a question re-

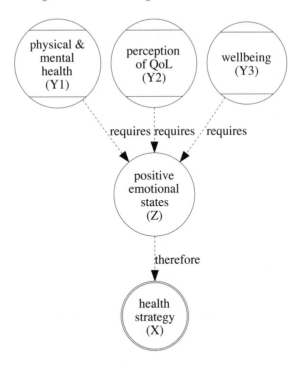

*Figure 6.3   Causal diagram of the function of the health policy; the elements
of the diagram are also marked in the XYZ typology*

mains: are the 'positive emotional states' sufficient to 'improve people's well-
being, their subjective perception of quality of life and their physical and mental health'? In a sense, we could be challenging the reasoning of the policy as
expressed in the text of Example 6.1 – Figure 6.5.

Figure 6.5 adds a second objective, 'good physical state' (Z2), which results
from an interpretation of the first of the two components of the first state of
interest (Y1): the physical part of health. This second objective also leads to
the formation of the health strategy (X), but now this strategy will have two
objectives to satisfy.

Figure 6.4   The terminology used in the hierarchy ranks may be confusing

6.2.5   Second Set of Diagrams

In the second set of diagrams we have the onus to seek the actions (X) that correspond to the objectives Z1 and Z2, and ultimately produce outcomes capable
of responding to the original three concerns (Y1–Y3). As per original terminology, we shall call the set of the resulting actions (X) the 'health strategy' –
Figure 6.6.

It seems that every aspect of the physical health is related to the emotional
side. Thus, in the more detailed action of the strategy (Figure 6.6) we merged
the two objectives Z1 and Z2, otherwise there was an unnecessary duplication
of links. Although we returned to having a single objective, this one is more
complete than the original, as it also contains the physical part of health.

The actions X1 through to X4 of the health strategy are general, in the sense
they all prescribe consultations by specialists, at recommended time intervals.
This suits the character of a health strategy, which remains general and does
not go into much detail.

The four actions were discovered through an analysis of the aspects of the
physical and emotional health, decomposing that into four 'specialities' and
recommending regular consultations. As in all cases of conceiving action, this
is also subject to debate and open to discussion. However, in the meantime
we know clearly – for instance through Figure 6.6 – the reasoning, or 'logical
causality' that led to the particular suggestion for action.

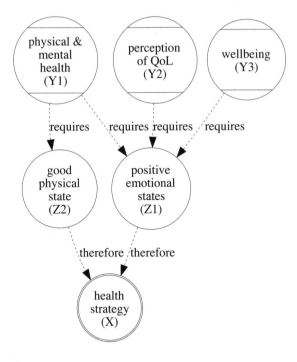

Figure 6.5   A challenge to the health policy; perhaps a second objective, Z2, focussing on physical health was missing from the original conception

The expected outcomes of the recommended action are 'all-round healthy individuals', based on the confidence that the regular consultations will monitor closely and care for the physical and mental health of the individuals. These outcomes satisfy not only the first, basic concern of physical and mental health (Y1), but also the perception of the quality of life (Y2) and wellbeing (Y3).

6.2.6 Notes

Following the loops in the health strategy (Figure 6.6), we notice that the original idea expressed in the text of Example 6.1 and depicted in Figure 6.2 is satisfied. This is a reassurance that our analysis and modifications produced a much clearer understanding of the content of the health strategy (called for by

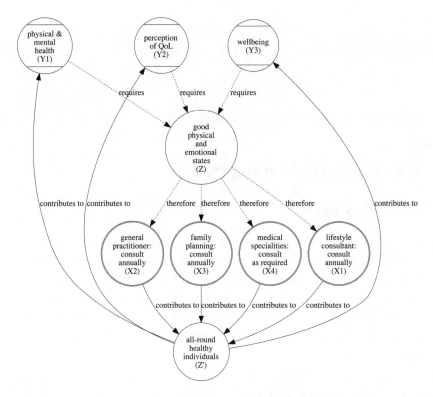

Figure 6.6   The health strategy

the health policy) without any distortion to or deviation from the original idea.

No side-effects are noted in the health strategy of Figure 6.6. If indicated in the original guideline as a condition or concern, we could have also indicated possible side-effects – for instance, the monetary costs of healthcare, and for whom these might incur.

The type of the health strategy problem is quite simple, following the basic sequence of $Y \to Z \to X \to Z' \to Y$ (Figure 6.7), which is one of the most effective and robust loops.

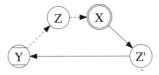

Figure 6.7   The type of the health strategy problem

6.3   Example: Housing Plan

6.3.1   Case Study

This case study is from a predominantly rural area in Norther Europe. The countryside is recognised to play an important role in the local quality of life. This housing attempt forms a plan of how the local authority (let us call it HDC) and its partners will meet the need for affordable housing in rural parts of their space. The plan was developed in consultation with a number of stakeholders and includes amendments to reflect the comments received through this.

6.3.2   Original Material

The rural housing strategy of HDC is structured in three levels: it starts with a general aim at the top rank, followed by a list of objectives, which are then followed by actions – or, rather, guidelines for action, as they are not directly executable. All relationships between the aim, objectives, and actions are clearly marked, not with the help of a diagram (which could be, for instance, a tree diagram), but in the form of lists. Example 6.2 is a self-contained extract that provides the working material for this section. Besides 'Objective A', there are another six objectives under the same aim. The three actions featured in this example represent the complete set for this objective.

The same information about action appears in a second source, namely in a table, replicated as Table 6.2. Although the first two actions are identical in the text and the table, the third action appears different – specifically, more detailed and executable in the table. This is noted as an inconsistency, as the actions cannot be trusted to be the same in the two sources. In fact, this is a case of duplication of references (specifically, of the action), which is capable of creating confusion and – in some cases – lack of coordination and errors.

Example 6.2   Rural Housing Plan – Extract

Aim of the strategy: To identify housing needs in the rural areas of the district and to work with partners to ensure those needs are met.

Objective A: To identify the specific needs of rural parishes and work with stakeholders to identify how to meet those needs.

Actions:

1. To use the housing register and housing needs surveys to identify Parishes with a housing need;

2. To develop homes to lifetime homes standard on schemes where specialised housing or housing for older people is identified;

3. To carry out publicity to encourage people in housing need to register on HDC's housing register.

6.3.3   First Set of Diagrams

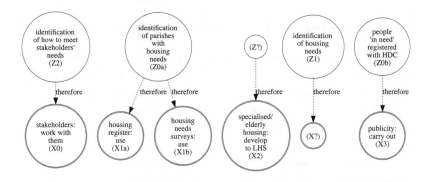

Figure 6.8   Causal map of the HDC plan, from the text of Example 6.2

Figure 6.8 presents the causal map of the HDC plan extract, created from the text of Example 6.2. Since the original text was not sufficiently clear, some

Table 6.2   A second source of the selected action of the housing strategy

Action	Target Date	Lead	Risk if not achieved	Links
To use the housing register and housing needs surveys to identify Parishes with a housing need	June 2007; every year	WP, HDC	Areas where there is a short-fall in afford-able housing will continue to have an unmet need	Homelessness Strategy, Housing Strategy, Parish Plans
To develop homes to life-time homes standard on schemes where specialised housing or housing for older people is identified	Every rural site given planning per-mission from 1 January 2007	WQ, H	Homes built for older peo-ple and/ or people with a specialised need cannot accommodate the residents when their need for adaptations or alterations arises	Housing Strategy, LDF
To produce an article to be published in Parish publi-cations and/or notice boards to encourage people in hous-ing need in the Parishes to reg-ister on HDC's housing register	Discuss ap-proach and content of article with Parishes by 14 March 2007. Article to be drafted by 1 April 2007. Article pub-lished by 30 June 2007	WP, HDC	A number of households in the Parishes in need of afford-able housing will miss the opportunity to access afford-able housing if they are not registered on HDC's Housing Waiting List	Housing Strategy, Parish Plans

transformations were necessary to produce the causal diagram. For instance, 'Objective A' was divided from the text into a Z1 and Z2, and the original expression was changed from verb ('to identify') to noun ('identification') for not confusing objectives as action.

6.3.4 Observations

The causal diagram of Figure 6.8) displays the correspondence between objectives and action, and this revealed more errors that were not detectable in the text of Example 6.2. In preparing the causal diagram, several errors became evident. First, two more objectives were discovered (Z0a and Z0b), as motives for action. Then, the objective Z1 did not appear to have an action associated with it, so it was like a dead-end. Moreover, the action X2 was not justified, since there was no objective associated with it. Finally, objective Z2 had a 'leftover' term that was prompting for action – namely, to work with the stakeholders; since this action was not part of the defined set, it was considered 'hidden' and marked as X0.

6.3.5 Second Set of Diagrams

The errors found in the original text and discovered in the first causal diagram had to be rectified. Thus, the second causal diagram (Figure 6.9) presents an improved expression of the original extract of the housing plan.

Figure 6.9 contains the two original objectives (Z1 and Z2). Action had to be reformulated to a great extent: X1 and X2 come from the original first action, and X3 comes from the original third action. The original second action gives rise to X4 (to seek solutions to housing needs within thinktanks), but action X4 depends on the outcomes (Z') of the other three actions, X1 to X3. Thus, here we evidence parallel actions (X1–X3) as well as sequential actions: X4 is executed after X1, X2, and X3 have produced outcomes.

6.3.6 Notes

Although the HDC plan appeared well structured in the original text, after some processing to produce causal diagrams revealed a number of deficiencies: uncertainty and omissions in the expression of the objectives and action; inconsis-

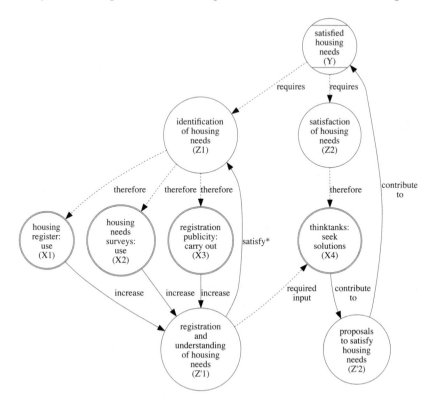

Figure 6.9   Improved proposal for the extract of the HDC housing plan

tency in the use of the words 'strategy' and 'plan'; and inconsistencies between text and table, as a result of double referencing. The construction of the XYZ diagram, as a graphical expression of the definition of the planning problem, gave an opportunity to correct the errors of the original planning effort.

The type of the planning problem in this case as expressed in Figure 6.10 is interesting due to the sequential action. In a sense, the planning problem has two parts (or branches, in the type diagram): the first is from the concern (Y) to the outcomes (Z′) of the first set of action (XI); the second features the second set of action (XII), which has two inputs: the objective Z2 as a motive and Z′ as material to process. Finally, the outcome of the second set of action (XII) is capable of satisfying the initial concern.

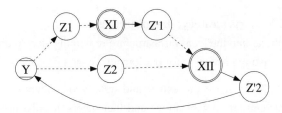

Figure 6.10   The type of the HDC housing problem

6.4   Example: Arts Strategy

6.4.1   Case Study

While 'development' in its classic interpretation is intimately related to space, more modern interpretations tend to accept more dimensions to development, as for example the theme of this case study: the arts. A local authority in Northern Europe – let us call it SLD – intends to promote the arts with a special strategy comprising of three aims and 13 'strategic objectives'. The strategy is conceived in a way that many of the objectives (divided under the three aims) are related to each other, and the achievement of one will support the achievement of others, as well. The interesting aspect of the SLD arts strategy is that the guidelines for action are not clearly marked in the text, so that practically the action is missing – thus we will have to deal with that here.

6.4.2   Original Material

To keep the example contained, let us select as our working text the first aim and the first objective – Example 6.3.

Example 6.3   Arts strategy: first objective

Aim 1: To strengthen the local infrastructure remaining alert to opportunities to enhance existing provision, for participants in, and producers of, the arts.

Objective 1: To increase the extent and quality of collaboration between SLD's artists and arts organisations and their peers, locally, regionally, nationally and internationally.

6.4.3   First Set of Diagrams

The attempt to create the first causal diagram follows the text closely, and turns out to be somewhat confusing as many ideas are lumped together – Figure 6.11.

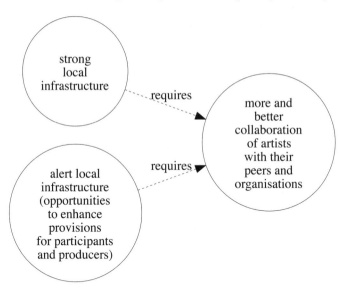

Figure 6.11   The first attempt to create a causal diagram of Example 6.3

The second attempt to create the causal diagram of Example 6.3 makes several interpretations guided by information contained in the broader documentation of the strategy, and uses an XYZ terminology and structure to clarify the information types and flows – Figure 6.12.

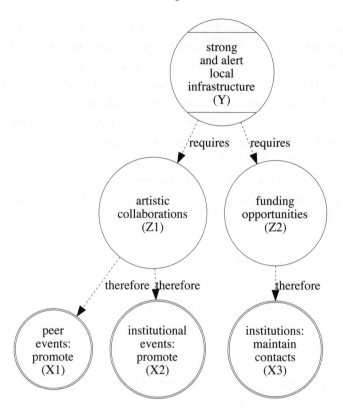

Figure 6.12   The second attempt to create the causal diagram

The core of the aim gives rise to the element of concern (Y), which can be expressed not only as a mere parameter, but including a definition of its current or desired state – in this case it is the desired state 'strong', which better guides the reasoning towards the objectives (Z1 and Z2).

6.4.4   Observations

Although the action of the strategy is technically missing – for instance, there is no heading marked as 'action' or 'measures' – we notice that both the aim and the objectives contain embedded action verbs: 'to strengthen', 'to enhance', 'to increase'. On one hand this 'embedded action' distorts the function of the strategy elements such as objectives (meaning that they do not express merely the intended states to achieve, but also the intended action with which to achieve the intended states), but on the other it helps us discover what the intended action is. This configuration is not very uncommon in the expression of strategies, and could represent the current trend or fashion, but its disorderly and – literally – 'confused' (from Latin *confundere*, meaning poured together or mixed up) arrangement leads the reader to not think clearly. Causal diagramming certainly helps to clarify the ideas, as for instance it gave assistance with the deciphering of the hidden action and permitted – albeit at a certain risk of having misinterpreted the original ideas – the definition of the three actions (X1 to X3) featured in Figure 6.12.

6.4.5 Second Set of Diagrams

After some extended reading, deciphering, and reasoning, we could produce the second causal diagram of the selected part of the arts strategy – Figure 6.13. In this diagram we notice the concrete outcomes, events and sponsorships, which help us comprehend the strategy somewhat better. This arrangement could give ideas for further outcomes, for instance of the quantitative nature that is popular in indicators of strategy success, such as funds raised or number of artists involved.

6.4.6 Notes

In this case study we saw that when the action is blended in together with the aims and objectives, and is not clearly marked, it may initially appear as missing. Some interpretation is then required to decipher what action is intended, which may be risky in the absence of the original plan authors. Even with this deficient information, it was possible to create a complete causal diagram for the planning problem in an XYZ form, which provided better understanding and a more clear plan.

The type of the planning problem in this case was a slight variation of the basic loop, featuring only one extra element (the second order outcomes, Z''). This does not indicate vulnerability of the plan, but rather its inherent complexity as the original concern was quite abstract, and so were the outcomes that were capable of satisfying it.

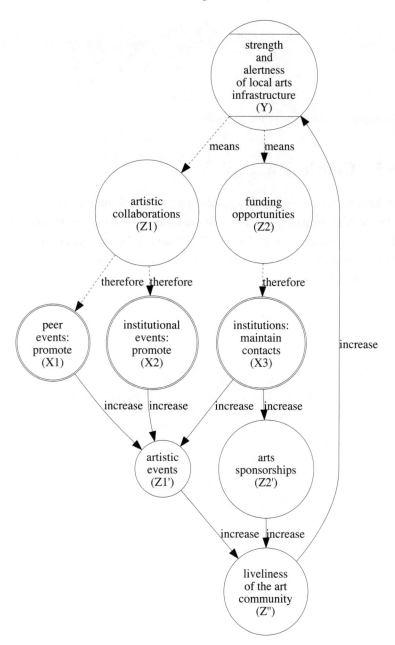

Figure 6.13   The arts plan in an XYZ form

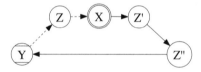

Figure 6.14   The type of the arts plan

6.5   Conclusion

In this chapter we learned how to discover the causal thinking in the original plan, with the help of descriptive causal diagrams (DCD) used in the context of descriptive causal analysis (DCA). The planning problem defaults to an XYZ form, as in the previous chapter regarding the creation of new plans, where we can verify and modify the action proposals when necessary.

7. Simulations

The examples presented in this chapter are also taken from case studies of existing action proposals, as in the previous chapter. The difference is that the proposals in this chapter are intended to remain as simulations, whose outcomes provide a base upon which to assess the proposals indirectly through their non-planned effects (or impacts). After the assessment, proposals for modification typically remain as minor modifications to the proposals, known as 'mitigations', while the opportunity to provide more substantial modifications to the original proposals still exists. The general area of this professional practice is known as 'impact assessment', and has evidenced many attempts – some with more success than others – for integration into planning, particularly through what is known as 'environmental planning'. In this chapter we shall have a brief view of what systems thinking has to offer to the 'effects specialists' of planning, and how we can link the effects studies to the planning problem.

Environmental impacts – or effects, as is the new tendency in the specialist technical nomenclature – are the unintended changes that human action causes to the environment, such as discharging high concentrations of combustion gases into the atmosphere or liquid industrial byproducts into waterways. Environmental impacts have been an apparent concern to humanity in recent years, as the natural environment is becoming increasingly more scarce and saturated to be able to absorb these changes. As a result, legislation to regulate environmental impacts has been in place in most countries, both at the strategic and the operational level – that is, respectively, for strategies such as plans and programmes, and investment projects.

The environmental impacts of strategic proposals such as plans and programmes are regulated by a process known as strategic environmental assessment (SEA), and those of investment projects by a process known as environmental impact assessment (EIA). The two processes are intended to communicate between them, and also integrate with the planning process – that is, the original creation of the action proposals. SEA tends to consider environmental impacts in a relatively broader view, without going into much depth, leaving the detailed analysis for the EIA process.

For the simulation of already defined proposals in this chapter we shall use the same process as defined in the previous chapter, and we shall also use diagrammatic causal diagrams (DCD) and analysis (DCA) to process the original material of the case studies. The information flow of the simulation is much simpler than a full planning problem, as illustrated in Figure 7.11. Typically we start with the action and seek a number of direct and indirect non-planned outcomes which must be assessed or evaluated – for instance, significant and negative, or positive but non-significant.

Figure 7.1   The information flow of a simulation has a limited scope, merely from action to outcomes

In Chapter 5 we encountered an example of qualitative simulation, illustrated in Figure 5.4, within the definition of a systems problem – that is, in an XYZ form. Equally for the simulations in this chapter, for the purposes of impact assessment, we will have to discover the original 'planning problem', in XYZ terms, which will provide the understanding regarding the extended mental model as well as the concrete physical and logical causality map (in a descriptive causal diagram form) on which we can make observations and modifications.

7.1   Example: Hydrocarbon Pollution

7.1.1   Case Study

Let us consider a case study from the environmental impact statement (EIS) of an investment project in transportation infrastructure. The selected text of Example 7.1 presents a proposal for remedial action – or mitigation – to compensate for forecasted environmental damage during the construction phase.

The issue of concern (Y) in this example is surface water quality.

7.1.2   Original Material

The original material from the case study is a brief but self-contained text extract, presented in Example 7.1.

Example 7.1   Plain text

In order to prevent hydrocarbons associated with construction traffic entering local watercourses a fabricated bypass petrol/oil interceptor should be installed upstream of attenuation ponds.

The text of Example 7.1 presents a mitigation measure for the investment project. We wish to examine (a) how, or in which mechanism the action is thought to bring about the expected outcomes, and (b) the structure of the planning problem (in this case, limited to the selected text), including why this action was proposed and whether the action is likely to achieve its intended outcomes.

Even with a brief extract, analysing the text for the above examination requires not only attention from the analyst, but also temporary memory to store the information while it is analysed. For larger extracts or complete proposals, the attention may remain the same but the memory requirements generally increase. To aid the process, and to be methodical, let us create a diagram from Example 7.1.

7.1.3   First Set of Diagrams

To prepare causal diagrams from text requires some processing, namely to mark the four semantics categories (Table 3.2) in the original text. Although it is possible to read the text and create a diagram at the same time (informally known as 'on the fly'), it is a good idea to mark the text before starting the diagram because that is more methodical, helps the memory retain information, and – most importantly – permits verification of all the reasoning as well as marking. In this example we shall use the text mark-up technique in Example

7.1, according to the conventions of Table 3.3. The output of the text mark-up operation is presented in Example 7.2.

Example 7.2 Marked text

In order to prevent HYDROCARBONS associated with CONSTRUCTION TRAFFIC entering LOCAL WATERCOURSES, a FABRICATED BYPASS PETROL/OIL INTERCEPTOR should be **installed upstream** of ATTENUATION PONDS.

Many technical descriptions that contain action, such as the above, are described as processes. If we follow the description of the 'action story' of Examples 7.1 or 7.2, it is very likely that our first diagram becomes a process diagram – namely, a concise process diagram (CPD) such as Figure 7.2.

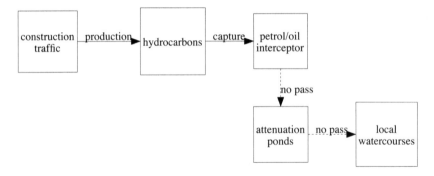

Figure 7.2   First diagram as a process, corresponding to Example 7.2

Process diagrams show how the action is carried out. For instance, in Figure 7.2 we can see how the hydrocarbons are produced from construction traffic and captured in the interceptor. After that, there should be no hydrocarbons found in the attenuation ponds, nor any in the local watercourses. However useful process diagrams may be for understanding the flow of hydrocarbons, though, they do not contribute much to the understanding of causes and effects. For instance, we cannot see the effect of the interceptor, but merely its function, which is to not allow hydrocarbons to pass beyond it (marked as 'no pass' on the arrow after the interceptor). In fact, process diagrams do not show effects at all: they merely show stages and actions – which we can also consider as 'operations' or 'functions'. To find out the effects, we need to produce a causal diagram – that is, a descriptive causal diagram (DCD) such as the one in Figure 7.3.

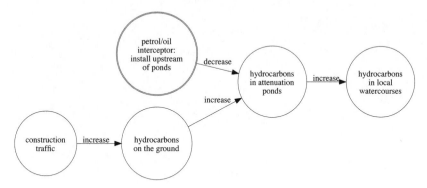

Figure 7.3   First causal diagram, corresponding to Example 7.2

The causal diagram of Figure 7.3 presents a different thinking than that of the previous figure. For instance, here we do not see how the hydrocarbons flow, but we see the effect of the interceptor, which is expected to decrease the amount of hydrocarbons in the attenuation ponds.

7.1.4   Observations

The preparation of the causal diagram required a little deviation from the terminology of the original text. As the process diagram was closer to the original text, perhaps it is a good idea to construct these two diagrams in the sequence presented here.

7.1.5   Second Set of Diagrams

The second causal diagram (Figure 7.4) is intended to correct any errors detected so far, to bring in clarifying information where doubts may exist, and – most importantly – identify and formalise the problem in an XYZ form.

Figure 7.4 presents the formal XYZ setup of the problem, including some modifications to the original plan which were discovered during the process-

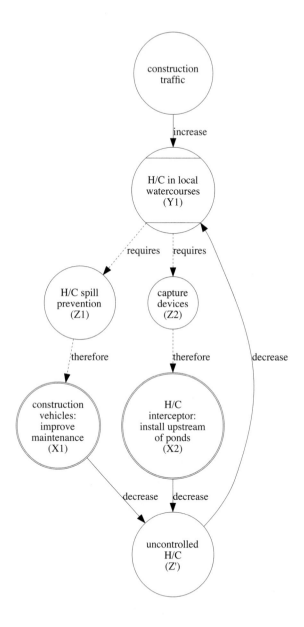

Figure 7.4   Second causal diagram, corresponding to Example 7.2

ing of the information. The issue of concern (Y) is identified as hydrocarbons (from the construction traffic) found in local watercourses. Since this should not be happening, hydrocarbons spills should be prevented (Z1) and, in case this is not perfectly successful, some capture devices should be installed in the right places (Z2). The first objective can be achieved by improving the status of vehicles (X1), for instance with better maintenance. The second objective can be achieved by installing a hydrocarbon interceptor upstream of the attenuation ponds (X2). Both of these actions are expected to contribute to reduce the uncontrolled, or spilled hydrocarbons (Z$'$), which should reduce the amount of hydrocarbons in the local watercourses, which was the issue of concern in this case.

7.1.6   Notes

The second causal diagram has added more actions to the original mitigation measures, so the text of the proposal is now presented as that of Example 7.3.

Example 7.3   Enhanced text

The issue of concern is the fact that hydrocarbons from the construction traffic make their way into local watercourses. Since this should not be happening, hydrocarbons spills should be prevented and, in case this is not perfectly successful, some capture devices should be installed in the right places. The first objective can be achieved by improving the status of vehicles with better maintenance. The second objective can be achieved by installing a hydrocarbon interceptor upstream of the attenuation ponds. Both of these actions are expected to contribute to reduce the uncontrolled, or spilled hydrocarbons, which should reduce the amount of hydrocarbons in the local watercourses. This is expected to improve the conditions regarding the issue of concern.

As a result of being produced after the causal diagram, the text of Example 7.3 is somewhat different in style (which is now causal) from the original text – which was expressed as a process. If necessary, this can be converted back into a process style, both in text and in diagram. Merely for illustration purposes, let us attempt to convert the 'causal' text or diagram into a 'process' version, featuring the alterations we made earlier – Figure 7.5.

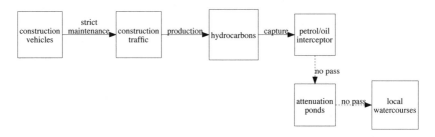

Figure 7.5   Introductory illustration: second diagram as a process, corresponding to Example 7.3

The new addition in the process is the 'vehicles' element, with an instruction for 'strict maintenance' before entering circulation. We verify once again that the process view is complementary to the causal view. If one of these diagrams should be used as a reference, then the other diagram should be clearly optional, or not exist at all, to avoid duplicate references.

The type of the illustrated causal diagram is quite simple, from concerns to objectives, to action, outcomes, and finally back to concerns (Figure 7.6).

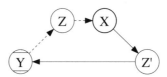

Figure 7.6   The type of the illustrated causal diagram

7.2   Example: Offshore Drilling

7.2.1   Case Study

In this example we work with an extract from an environmental impact statement (EIS), regarding the detailed analysis of the environmental impacts of an investment project. The case study is an offshore petroleum drilling project, and the particular extract deems the air emissions as not significant for the local environment, due to wind action in the area, and as extremely small on a continental scale. Based on the precautionary principle, we will try to improve practice with mitigation measures that are simple and not very costly.

7.2.2   Original Material

The extract presented in Example 7.4 is concerned with the air emissions from the operations of the project, as well as with the consequences of these emissions. The text contains forecasting, such as the generation of air emissions, although the quantitative estimates are referred to in another section, and also assessment of impacts – for instance, issuing judgements such as 'negligible' or 'extremely small'.

Example 7.4   Environmental Impacts

Emissions to air are generated primarily by the burning of fuel to power the engines, compressors and generators on the drilling unit and vessels. It is generally accepted that such emissions will be rapidly dispersed. Therefore, there is likely to be negligible contamination of the local environment due to dispersal and dilution by wind. Gases such as carbon dioxide and nitrogen oxides emitted during the course of the survey contribute to global warming although the contributions are extremely small when considered on a continental scale.

7.2.3   First Set of Diagrams

The text of Example 7.4 is written very close to a description of a process diagram, which may reveal a similar type of thinking from the engineering team who wrote the environmental impact statement – with possible origins in the formulation of the project proposal. We verify that enough information exists to create a process diagram – Figure 7.7.

The starred expressions are assessments or evaluations, as originally made in the environmental impact statement. The dashed lines represent the contribution of air emissions to global air pollution as being insignificant, as stated in

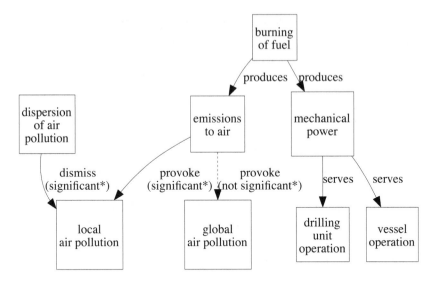

Figure 7.7   Process diagram corresponding to Example 7.4

the text extract. The contribution of air emissions to local air pollution is significant, but counter-balanced by the also significant cleaning effect (dispersion) of the air pollution by the wind action.

Now let us create a causal diagram from the process diagram. This is shown in Figure 7.8. In this conversion we also begin to label the diagram elements in terms of problem structure – that is, in XYZ terms. It becomes obvious that the wind (Y) is a 'significant condition' in this case (not as a concern this time, but rather as a solution), as it is essential to provide the mitigation for the local impacts, namely to reduce the local air pollution.

The causal diagram of Figure 7.8 features no dashed lines, but the overall significance of the effects is determined at the receptor ends, aligned by the lower part of the diagram: local and global air pollution. For instance, local air pollution receives two inputs: a significant increase from the project and a significant decrease from the wind; thus, the overall effect is not significant, as one effect counterbalances the other – always according to the environmental impact statement.

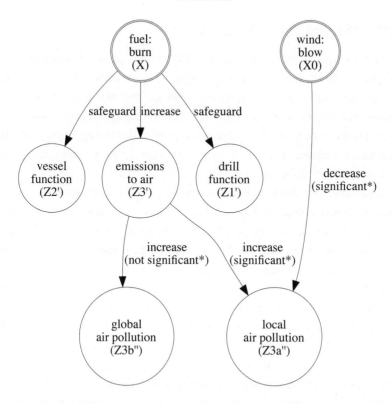

Figure 7.8   Causal diagram corresponding to Example 7.4

7.2.4   Observations

So far we have an idea about the function of some system elements in terms of a problem, in XYZ terms, but this is not complete yet. As per procedure, we will come to that in the second set of diagrams.

Although the assessment of the forecast impacts renders them as non significant, we can still explore the possibility of taking precautions to lower air emissions with mitigations that may not mean a considerable investment. Thus, in one of the next diagrams we must also think of possible mitigations to the adverse effects, which are 'emissions to air', not leaving everything to the wind to resolve – perhaps something along the lines of combustion efficiency.

7.2.5   Second Set of Diagrams

Figure 7.9 presents the full problem in XYZ formulation, but no human mitigation yet. In this diagram we can see the origin of the described issue, namely the drilling operation, as well as its two main objectives: to secure a drilling unit and vessels for transportation purposes. The drilling unit and the vessels are united here, in their common characteristic which is that they employ internal combustion engines. Thus, we identify our target for human-made mitigation as is the first side effect of the combustion, namely air emissions (Z').

After the full definition of the problem, Figure 7.10 presents some further mitigation actions that aim to reduce air emissions. This environmental objective ($Z3$) is requested at the same level as the main objectives of the drilling operation, namely securing a drilling unit and support vessels. In this sense, the project (at least in this demonstrated part) features now a built in environmental objective.

Figure 7.10 also explores what this environmental objective may mean in practice. For instance, as demonstrated here, it could imply (a) purchasing fuel with lower sulfur content, to reduce the sulfur oxide emissions, (b) running the engines at lower temperatures, for instance using larger cooling units, or others that could make use of the nearby sea water, in order to reduce the nitrogen oxide emissions, and (c) have catalysts installed in the exhaust pipes of the engines. Although there are costs involved with any of these mitigation measures, they appear capable of reducing the air emissions below the level of the 'do nothing' option.

7.2.6   Notes

The extract of the offshore drilling project, concerned with air emissions from two main operations of the project (drilling and local maritime transport), illustrated that the expression of forecasts and assessments, which are typical in the content of EIA, can be represented together (but distinctly) in causal diagrams, and thus they are communicated more clearly than in text.

When thinking of mitigation measures, it is possible to incorporate environmental objectives in the project by taking the original objectives one level more abstract – or hierarchically higher. This is feasible by gaining an integrated 'problem view' in an XYZ form, as in Figures 7.9 and 7.10. Incorporat-

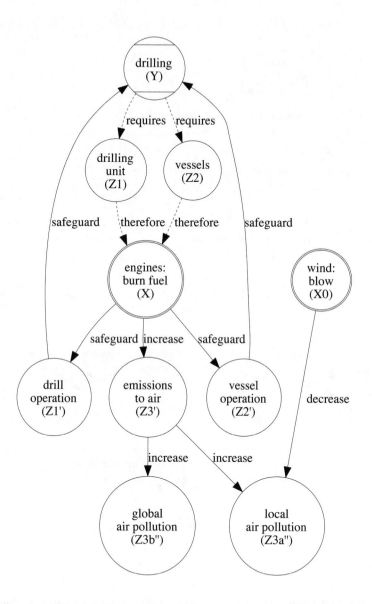

Figure 7.9   Causal diagram of the second set, corresponding to Example 7.4

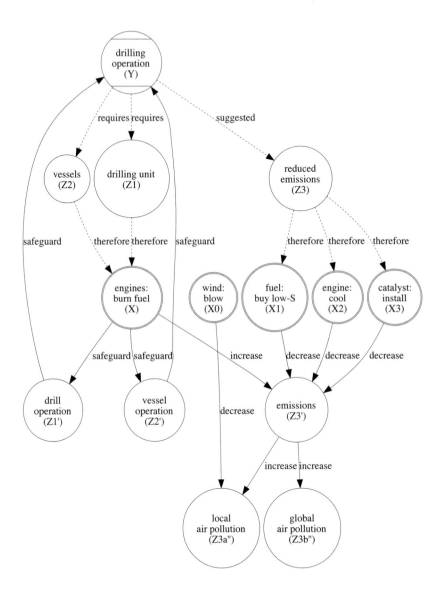

Figure 7.10   Enhanced causal diagram of the second set, featuring extended solutions (actions X1 to X3)

ing environmental objectives instead of proposing 'end of the pipe' technical mitigations makes the action proposal pro-active rather than re-active, and thus intrinsically more benign. Thus, when environmental objectives are incorporated into the action proposal, then mitigation measures for reducing identified adverse impacts result from within – from the (new) environmental objective. In either way, it is always a good idea to simulate the suggested mitigation measures, to make sure they contribute to the attenuation of the forecasted adverse effect of the project.

The causal diagrams of the second set do not have markings of significance next to the effects, as an option to keep the diagrams simple. As we saw in the first causal diagram, it is possible to mark the significance (or non-significance) in text, but other options could also be used – for instance symbols, colours, or variations of the arrows that carry this information.

The transcription of the text of Example 7.4 to a diagram (in this case first to a process diagram) was carried out mentally – that is, not using text mark-up in the analysis of semantics. This procedure is capable of producing diagrams faster, but the verification of correctness is not easy – it is almost as onerous as repeating the transcription.

The type of the XYZ problem is a basic loop, with the environmental concerns of the side-effects (Z'') being mitigated internally (through X and Z') and externally, through X0.

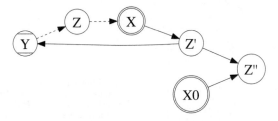

Figure 7.11   The type of the drilling operation problem

7.3   Example: Transport Plan

7.3.1   Case Study

This is an example of strategic environmental assessment (SEA), illustrated with a case study of a local transport plan (LTP) from a local authority in Europe that employs causal diagrams to present how the proposed actions are expected to satisfy their objectives, as well as how environmental effects are thought to arise. Given this opportunity of a diagrammatic expression of causal thinking in practice, the base for the working example is a sample of the original causal diagram: the simulation of a transport plan.

7.3.2   Original Material

Figure 7.12 presents a self-contained extract from the strategic environmental assessment (SEA) of the local transport plan (LTP). The diagram starts with what could be the conceived action on the left-hand side (although this is not clearly labelled) and ends with the outcomes on the right-hand side – although instead of the planned outcomes, which we usually designate as Z', in the diagram we have their mirror images: the aims of the strategy, which we would designate as Z (being the same type as, or perhaps in lieu of objectives).

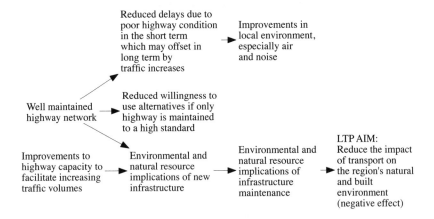

Figure 7.12   An extract from the original diagram

Starting the exploration with a new medium – that is, other than running text – let us make some preliminary observations before proceeding with the causal diagrams.

Contrary to the aim of the LTP extract, which is clearly marked in the last block of Figure 7.12, the action proposed by the plan is not marked in the diagram. It is to be deduced that the action proposals stand at the origin of the cause-and-effect sequences – that is, on the left side of the diagram. However, upon closer inspection, only the lower text block resembles a proposed action; the upper block ('well maintained highway network') is either a fact, a hypothesis, or an objective to achieve.

The final effect on the aim of the LTP is marked as 'negative', which transmits sufficient information to the SEA specialists, but this refers to the global effect of all inputs (or influences) to the aim. For instance, if there were more inputs to the same aim, we would not know the type of influence of each one of them (such as positive or negative) on the aim, but only the overall effect marked inside the text block. This is not necessarily undesirable, but it is not as analytic as the conventions of Chapter 4 permit.

The text is abundant, but contains some inconsistencies. One of the intermediate blocks that present the intermediate outcomes or effects has the same expression ('improvements') as the original action, on the left hand side of the original diagram, so there is some confusion here as to whether or not they are both of the same semantic category. The intermediate effects are forecasted and marked clearly such as 'reduced delays' or 'reduced willingness', but there is no assessment of these changes – for instance, reduced delays are unwanted, or negative effects.

7.3.3   First Set of Diagrams

Based on the above observations, we translate the original diagram of Figure 7.12 into a descriptive causal diagram – Figure 7.13.

7.3.4   Observations

In creating the causal diagram of Figure 7.13 it was necessary to make some changes to the original diagram, such as shorten the text expressions, classify them in terms of their function (in XYZ terms), and reduce some uncertainty

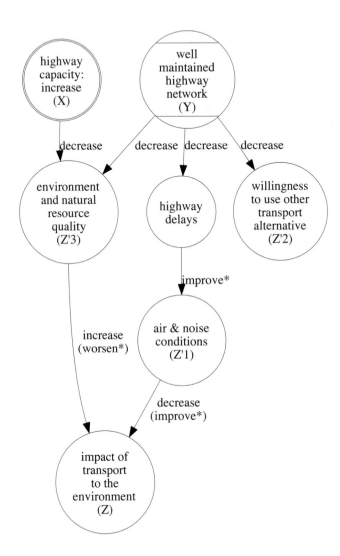

Figure 7.13   A causal diagram for the LTP extract, produced from Figure 7.12 with a number of observations and interpretations

(for instance in the $Z'3$ element). In more detail, the following changes provided more insight into the simulation.

The 'well maintained highway network' is taken as an initial condition. This serves well the case of the simulation of a particular scenario – for instance, 'catering for the car', where the original diagram came from. Therefore, it is labelled in Figure 7.13 as 'Y'.

There are two environmental effects ($Z'1$ and $Z'3$), on different aspects of the environment (whether or not this was intentional in the original diagram), and here we directed them both to the original aim (Z). As one improves and the other worsens the impact of transport on the environment, it will have to be determined (perhaps scientifically) what the overall effect is. Here we merely report the expected contributions.

As a technical note, the last two effects marked on the two arrows by the right hand side of Figure 7.13 transmit information objectively and subjectively – that is, after an assessment against certain values. For instance, the improved air and noise conditions ($Z'1$) decrease – which in our case means improve – the impact of transport on the environment (Z).

7.3.5   Second Set of Diagrams

Strategic environmental assessment (SEA) is typically called to assess a given action proposal, or a set of alternatives, with the possibility to start this work during the elaboration of the proposal. Whether it is up to the SEA or the planning team, or jointly, there is an opportunity to shape the plan to conform to a number of environmental objectives. While there are many ways to discover the action that would permit that, let us consider a technique based on the work we have carried out so far.

If we have explored the causal pathways from action to outcomes such as aims or objectives, effects, or impacts (Figure 7.13), we can also go the opposite way: start from desired outcomes, such as the desired environmental state, to discover the action of the plan that would achieve that. Figure 7.14 presents a diagram that proceeds in the reverse direction to that of Figure 7.13.

Although the diagram of Figure 7.14 is subjective, and anyone would come up with a different version (for instance based on experience, knowledge, or imagination), it has the value of organised and registered thinking in 'logical

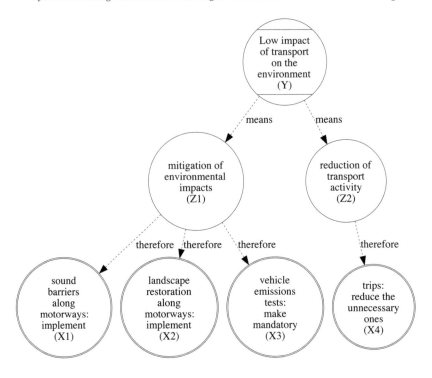

Figure 7.14 Reverse diagram (objectives to action)

causality' that can lead us to conceive the action of the plan. Being registered, the reasoning and arguments can be debated among all interested (and invited) parties, rather than anyone imposing their own ideas on anyone else without any clear explanation. While even debates can fail, especially if not moderated well, setting the objectives in a shared environment and searching for the solutions (actions) together is a great advance towards openness and transparency.

The value of this 'reverse' causal diagram can be appreciated in particular when by setting an environmental vision (or a part of it, in this example), we start unfolding the reasoning for what that means, which can help us discover the objectives, and then continue the search for what to do in order to achieve these objectives – which is precisely the action, or the solution to the problem. The scope of this search is adjustable, but some training (or coaching, especially in the beginning) is necessary in order not to get too enthusiastic and fill up pages and pages of vision elements and objectives – in which the team can easily get lost or confused and lose interest.

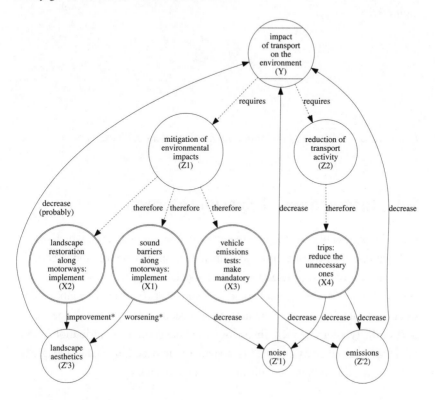

Figure 7.15   Final (complete) reverse diagram of the LTP

7.3.6   Notes

When SEA employs this kind of systems thinking to set up problems and work with causal diagrams, this can serve the basic function of SEA (that is, the forecasting and assessment part), but can take the extra step and make the SEA suggestions more creative – although this could set back the original planners. Therefore, this complete contribution of SEA to planning is best applied when the SEA team is invited at an early stage to work together with the planners. So far, systems thinking is available for (and accessible to) both the SEA and the planning practitioners and consultants, as demonstrated in this book.

The type of the planning problem of the LTP extract is the basic loop – Figure 7.16.

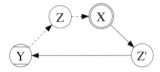

Figure 7.16   The type of the planning problem of the LTP extract

7.4   Interactions of Special Interest

From the perspective of studying the effects of action proposals, which occurs in the practice of environmental assessment (European Commission, 1999), for instance, two types of interactions are of special interest: (a) those that occur one after the other, sequentially, and (b) those that occur from combinations, whether of actions or other impacts. In this section we provide a brief highlight of the typology of these interactions and the potential contribution of diagrammatic causal analysis (DCA) – together with descriptive causal diagrams (DCD) – regarding their identification and understanding.

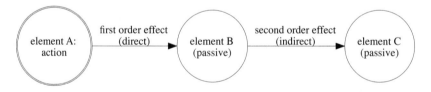

Figure 7.17   Generic diagram regarding direct and indirect effects

The first type of the interactions of special interest regards the 'causal order' of effects – for instance, whether they are direct (that is, of first order) or indirect (that is, of second or higher order) – Figure 7.17.

Figure 7.18 presents an illustration from a case study to demonstrate the fact that many important system elements (or parameters), such as water quality or fauna and flora, are usually quite remote from the action in terms of causal order, but still get affected to an extent that often causes concern – for instance, regarding pollution.

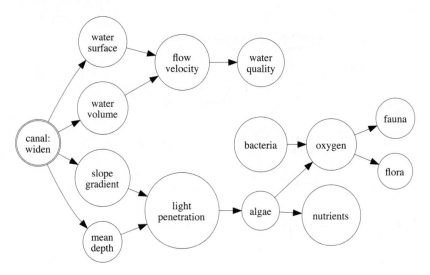

Figure 7.18   Many important system elements are usually quite remote from the action in terms of causal order

As a technical note, no effects are marked on the causality arrows of Figure 7.18 because in the original material of the case study only some effects were properly identified as 'increase' or 'decrease'. The rest were referred to in an ambiguous manner, for instance such as 'changes' or 'affects'. The omission of the labelling of the effects is not relevant for the purposes of this illustration, as the importance is to identify the order of the effects rather than the trends.

The second type of the interactions of special interest regards the 'merging' of information, and relates to cumulative effects – that is, effects that result from incremental changes caused by past, present and/or foreseeable actions (Figure 7.19) – and effect interactions (Figure 7.20).

When information from two or more elements merges into a new element, it becomes difficult to predict what is likely to happen. When information is quantitative – as often happens in system dynamics modelling, for instance – forecasting may be somewhat less challenging because the mathematical func-

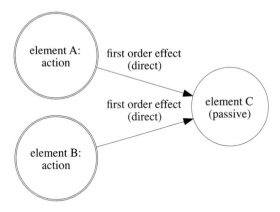

Figure 7.19   Generic diagram regarding cumulative effects

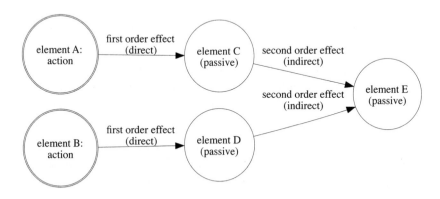

Figure 7.20   Generic diagram regarding effect interactions

tions are relatively easy to define, data is relatively easy to input, and the processing is done by a computer. When information is qualitative, as is often the
case in planning and always the case with descriptive causal diagrams (DCD),
the information processing – or thinking, in this case – regarding forecasts
must be done mentally by the planners and their consultants, with 'manual'
assistance by the diagrams.

For instance, Figure 7.21 presents a causal diagram created from one of the
many instances of reporting cumulative effects between existing action and the
proposal of new action. While the pathway of the effect is made clear with the
help of the diagram, forecasts are still a challenge.

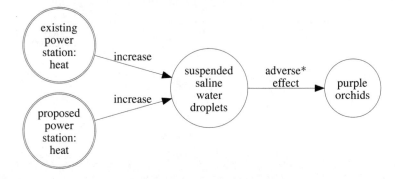

*Figure 7.21   An existing and a proposed action are expected to have cumula-
tive effects*

Figure 7.22 presents a somewhat more complex example from another case
study. The diagram starts with four environmental effects directly caused by
the action (also known as 'first order' or 'direct' effects), which interact to
ultimately affect biodiversity – that is, an aspect of the system that is generally
considered important – in a negative way.

In complex cases with multiple inputs and interactions, we usually have to
make simplifications before discovering clear patterns of how the effects shape
– and always with care not to manipulate the information so that it 'fits' a
particular pattern we wish to work with, or not to produce a 'black box' by
reducing excessively. Processing this information with the assistance of causal
diagrams is easier than without it, but still there is a skill to perfect through

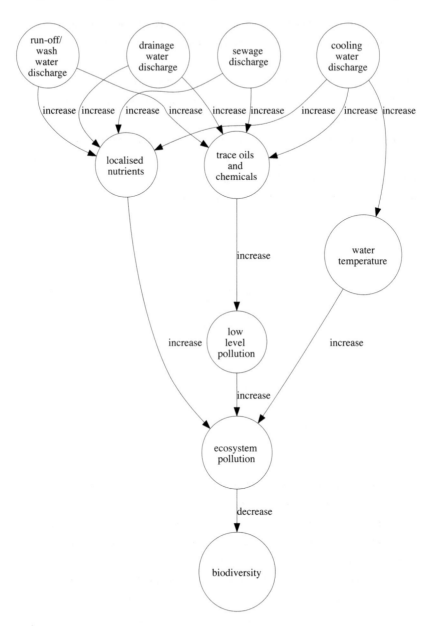

Figure 7.22   Important aspects of the system of interest are usually the products of interactions between effects of various orders

practice: the art of systems modelling.

7.5 Conclusion

In this chapter we considered the examination and modification of existing action proposals within the professional practice of impact assessment – for instance environmental impact assessment (EIA) and strategic environmental assessment (SEA). We went beyond the basic requirement of simulation of the action proposals by discovering and understanding the extended mental model of the interventions as a complete planning problem, in XYZ terms, in which operation the descriptive causal diagrams (DCD) and causal analysis (DCA) were essential. The feedback of impact assessment into planning is a long-standing item on the 'to do' list, and finds a practical implementation with the methods and techniques presented in this book.

Epilogue

It is efficient to think clearly and focus on what matters, as well as to share and communicate that with those who matter. Building on prior systems thinking advances, we reviewed ways to 'see' the hidden elements and forces behind both the planned and consequential changes in urban and environmental systems. We can express, check, and fine-tune our 'restricted' mental models about the structure and function of target systems with explicit cause-and-effect relationships.

With the new contribution of systems thinking in planning made in this book, we can train our systems thinking skills to express our planning problems as 'extended' mental models, featuring the concerns (Y), the objectives (Z) we define, and the action (X) that is capable of satisfying these objectives. Thus, the structural and functional organisation of the target systems extends into the planning process.

This advance introduces a particular formality to urban and environmental planning with regards to the expression of action and associated information such as concerns, objectives, and outcomes. Expressing the planning problem in the form of causal diagrams creates a new kind of 'maps', which could begin to be a standard appendix to new plans, or an addendum to revisions of older plans – approximately similar in size and degree of specialisation to the indispensable geographic maps.

Alea iacta est. There is plenty of work to be done, and systems thinking is quite special – in planning and beyond: it is 'different thinking', efficient, and deeply satisfying.

Glossary

Note

Terminology in planning tends to be somewhat inconsistent. Under the general idea that languages and professions evolve, this is not worrying. In practical terms, though, words manage to have different meanings and uses across time, space, and across cultures – even if the language is the same – which makes consulting glossaries quite important. For instance, for some people 'goal' is more specific than 'objective', while for others it is the other way around.

This glossary has been prepared to provide: (a) the most precise definitions for the entries, which means they are internally consistent within the book; (b) the most accurate definitions, corresponding to the 'real world', and for this we always check with the root or the origin of the words; and (c) the most up to date explanations for the listed entries, checking with external current references such as planning literature and dictionaries.

Definitions and Explanations

Aim   (n.) An intention; a synonym of 'objective', as something we wish to achieve, but more general or abstract.

Assessment   Determine the importance, size, or value of something; set a value on real or personal property, usually for purposes of taxation; from *assidere* (L.) – sit beside, assist [in the office of a judge].

Causality   The relationship between causes and effects; sometimes the same notion appears as 'causation', especially in older texts, but 'causation' is closer to 'causing an action' rather than indicating a relationship.

Criterion   (plural: criteria; from Greek χρίσις – judgement) Reference by which we can make a judgement.

Decision   Conclusion or resolution reached after consideration; choice (and fixing of that choice) made after thinking and talking about what is the best thing to do. Originally: 'cut-off' – from Latin *de-* (off) and *caedere* (to cut).

Development   A specified state of growth or advancement, or the process of reaching that state; the word has a common root with 'envelope' (of unknown origin); development can be used with 'pre-programmed' systems, such as living organisms (that is, with their development encoded in the DNA), but not with non-living systems such as the Earth.

Dynamics   Relationships between entities, in a way that one 'forces' the other to behave in a certain way – from Greek δύναμις (force).

EIA   (Environmental Impact Assessment) Process that identifies, forecasts, evaluates, and suggests mitigation of the (biophysical, social, and other relevant) effects of development proposals prior to major decisions being taken and commitments made.

Goal   A desired achievement. In this book, as in most of the business planning literature, goals are expressed in more concrete terms than objectives, so they describe the specific and often measurable results (or outcomes) the organisation intends to achieve. McLoughlin (1969), in contrast, considers goals as more abstract than objectives.

Heuristics   Type of techniques that enable a person to discover (from Greek ευρίσχειν – to find) or learn something for themselves, often by trial and error or by rules that are only loosely defined.

Index
(pl. indices) A composite expression with a unidimensional value (often unit-less), reflecting the status of a complex object or situation. Indices typically combine a number of parameters, thus funnelling a number of dimensions of complexity into a single dimension. Indices are often mathematical combinations of indicators, and may be objective (simply combining facts) or subjective (for instance, incorporating comparisons to values of reference).

Indicator
A quantifiable (and preferably measurable) parameter of a complex object or situation, typically reflecting one dimension of its status. Indicators can be combined to form indices.

Judgement
A considered decision or conclusion such as a classification, made against some reference criteria – for instance, preferences or laws.

Mental models
Thematic cognitive maps based on understanding and knowledge, but also containing assumptions and generalisations; they influence how we see and understand the world, as well as how we reach conclusions and take action.

Method
An established procedure for doing something within a known context – from Greek μετά + οδός, which means 'returning to the [known] path' or 'marking the path [for finding it again]'; contrast strategy.

Objective
(n.) A desired outcome in general terms; it can be specified further (see goals and targets).

Plan
Action proposal at the second highest tier of strategy, between policy and programme; also a generic form to express 'what to do' (for a particular, yet often implicit purpose).

Planning	The operation of preparing for the future; the procedure varies in protocol and degrees of complexity and rigour; the 'spatial' version has a strong interest in actions regarding the organisation of space, including the built and the natural environment.
Policy	Action proposal at the highest tier of strategy; also, a generic form to indicate action, or a principle of action.
Problem	A question thrown forward – from Greek πρόβλημα (from πρό, forward + βάλλειν, to throw, as in 'ballistics'). The original idea about 'problems' was that if someone threw a question forward, then someone might answer it.
Programme	Action proposal at the lower tier of strategy, and one tier above the operational level.
Project	Action at the operational (or tactic) level; it may arise from strategic tiers (top-down approach), or may be conceived before them (bottom-up approach).
Rational	Using reason or logic in thinking out a problem; in accordance with the principles of logic or reason.
Reason	The faculty of rational argument, deduction, judgment, etc.; the power of comprehending, inferring, or thinking especially in orderly (rational) ways.
Scope	The angle in which we are looking (see Aim); it determines how many things we see when we look.
SEA	(Strategic Environmental Assessment) Process that analyses and assesses strategy proposals; facilitates the search for the best option and supports democratic decision making; can be combined with impact assessment at the project level (that is, EIA).
Semantics	The meaning of a word, sentence, etc. (from Greek σημαντικός 'significant', from σημαίνειν 'signify', from σημα 'sign').

Strategic planning	A planning method (that is, a way to plan); credited to the ancient Greek military (στρατός); in the early 20th C., it became popular in the private sector (that is, businesses), and later appeared in the public sector – including spatial planning.
Strategy	An action proposed to achieve an intended outcome; strategy is high-level and abstract, condensed, or generalized action; strategy is pioneering action, confronting novel situations and unexplored grounds; therefore, it contains risks and can follow no pro-forma instructions (recipes) – from Greek στρατός + άγειν, which means 'leading the army [in new and unknown conditions]').
SWOT	A diagnostic technique that identifies strengths, weaknesses, opportunities and threats for a particular situation. The technique classifies facts into these four categories with reference to one or more specific objectives.
System	A set of connected things or parts forming a complex whole, in particular; a set of things working together as parts of a mechanism or an interconnecting network.
Target	An intended outcome, usually defined with time deadlines and quantitative achievement marks.
Theory	A generally accepted 'view' or mental map (system of ideas intended to explain something), usually verified with experimental confirmation; from Greek θεωρία (contemplation, speculation), associated to θεωρός (spectator).
Values	What is important to an organisation, a community, etc.
Vision	A conceived image of a state (most commonly about the future, but it can also be about the past), highly condensed or concentrated.

Bibliography

Adin, E.K. (2003), Planning in the Dark: Russian Planning Beneath the Iron Curtain, *Plan*, (Autumn):37–40.

Albers, G. (2006), Urban development, maintenance and conservation: planning in Germany – values in transition, *Planning Perspectives*, **21**:45–65.

Albrechts, L. (2001), In Pursuit of New Approaches to Strategic Spatial Planning: A European Perspective, *International Planning Studies*, **6**(3):293–310.

Albrechts, L. (2004), Strategic (spatial) planning reexamined, *Environment and Planning B: Planning and Design*, **31**:743–758.

Alexander, E.R. (1992), *Approaches to Planning: Introducing Current Planning Theories, Concepts and Issues* (2nd ed.), Philadelphia, PA: Gordon and Breach Science Publishers.

Allmendinger, P. (2002a), *Planning Theory*, Basingstoke, Hampshire: Palgrave.

Allmendinger, P. (2002b), Towards a Post-Positivist Typology of Planning Theory, *Planning Theory*, **1**(1):77–99.

Archibugi, F. (2004), Planning Theory: Reconstruction or Requiem for Planning? *European Planning Studies*, **12**(3):425–445.

Argyris, C. (1985), *Strategy, Change, and Defensive Routines*, Boston: Pitman.

Axelrod, R., (1976), *Structure of Decision: the Cognitive Maps of Political Elites*, Princeton, NJ: Princeton University Press.

Barrow, C.J. (1994), *Developing the Environment: Problems & Management*, Harlow, Essex: Longman Scientific & Technical.

Bartuska, T.J., and G.L. Young (eds), (1994), *The Built Environment: A Creative Inquiry into Design & Planning*, Menlo Park, CA: Crisp Publications.

Batty, M. (1976), *Urban Modelling: Algorithms, Calibrations, Predictions*, Cambridge: Cambridge University Press.

Baum, H.S. (1983), *Planners and Public Expectations*, Cambridge, MA: Schenkman.

Bernstein, D.J. (2001), Local government measurement use to focus on performance and results, *Evaluation and Program Planning*, **24**:95–101.

Blackerby, P. (1994), Strategic Planning: an overview for complying with GPRA, *Armed Forces Comptroller*, **39**:17–22.

Boardman, P. (1978), *The Worlds of Patrick Geddes: Biologist, Town Planner, Re-educator, Peace-warrior*, London: Routledge & Kegan Paul.

Bono, E. de (1996), *Teach Yourself to Think: Five Easy Steps to Direct, Productive Thinking*, London: Penguin Books.

Bradford, R.W., and J.P. Duncan (2000), *Simplified Strategic Planning: A No-Nonsense Guide for Busy People Who Want Results Fast!*, Worcester, MA: Chandler House Press.

Breheny, M., and A. Hooper (eds) (1985), *Rationality in Planning: Critical Essays on the Role of Rationality in Urban & Regional Planning*, London: Pion.

Bruton, M., and D. Nicholson (1987), *Local Planning in Practice*, Leckhampton: Stanley Thornes.

Bryson, J.M. (1995), *Strategic Planning for Public and Nonprofit Organizations: a Guide to Strengthening and Sustaining Organizational Achievement*, San Francisco: Jossey–Bass.

Bryson, J.M., F. Ackerman, and C. Eden (2007), Putting the Resource-Based View of Strategy and Distinctive Competencies to Work in Public Organizations, *Public Administration Review*, **July–August**:702–717.

Carmona, M. (2003), An International Perspective on Measuring Quality in Planning, *Built Environment*, **29**(4):281–287.

CCRE – Conseil des Communes et Régions D'Europe (1994), *Guide pour la réalization des plans stratégiques de développement des villes moyennes*, Lisbon: Officina de Arquitectura.

Chadwick, G.F. (1966) A Systems View of Planning, *Journal of the Town Planning Institute*, **52**:184–186.

Chadwick, G. (1971), *A Systems View of Planning: Towards a Theory of the Urban and Regional Planning Process* (1st ed.), Oxford: Pergamon Press.

Chadwick, G. (1978), *A Systems View of Planning: Towards a Theory of the Urban and Regional Planning Process* (2nd ed.), Oxford: Pergamon Press.

Chadwick, G.F. (1987), *Models of Urban and Regional Systems in Developing Countries: Some Theories and their Application in Physical Planning*,

Oxford: Pergamon Press.

Chalmers, A.F. (1999), *What is this thing called Science?* (3rd ed.), Buckingham: Open University Press.

Chapin, F.S. Jr. (1962) *Urban Land Use Planning*, Urbana, Illinois.

Checkland, P. (1981), *Systems Thinking, Systems Practice*, Chichester: John Wiley.

Checkland, P. (2000), Soft Systems Methodology: a Thirty Year Retrospective. *Systems Research and Behavioral Science*, **17**:11–58.

Checkland, P., and S. Holwell (1998), *Information, Systems and Information Systems*, Chichester: John Wiley.

Checkland, P., and J. Scholes (1990), *Soft Systems Methodology in Action*, Chichester: John Wiley.

Chermack, T.J. (2004), Improving decision-making with scenario planning, *Futures*, **36**:295–309.

Cooper, L.M., and W.R. Sheate (2004), Integrating Cumulative Effects Assessment into UK Strategic Planning: Implications of the European Union SEA Directive, *Impact Assessment and Project Appraisal*, **22**(5):5–16.

Cullingworth, J.B. (1970), *Town and Country Planning in England and Wales: the Changing Scene* (3rd ed.), London: George Allen & Unwin.

Cullingworth, J.B. (2009), *Planning in the USA: Policies, Issues, and Processes* (3rd ed.), Abingdon: Routledge.

Cullingworth, J.B., and V. Nadin (1994), *Town & Country Planning in Britain* (11th ed.), London: Routledge.

Dale, R. (2004), *Development Planning: Concepts and Tools for Planners, Managers and Facilitators*, London: Zed Books.

Dawes, R.M. (1988), *Rational Choice in an Uncertain World*, Orlando, FL: Harcourt Brace College Publishers.

ECFESD – European Consultative Forum on Environment and Sustainable Development (1999), *The European Spatial Development Perspective – ESDP*, Brussels: European Commission.

EEA (2005), *EEA Core Set of Indicators: Guide – EEA Technical report 1/2005*, Copenhagen: European Environment Agency.

Esty, D.C., M. Levy, T. Srebotnjak, and A. Sherbinin (2005), *2005 Environmental Sustainability Index: Benchmarking National Environmental Stewardship*, New Haven: Yale Center for Environmental Law & Policy.

European Commission (1997), *The EU compendium of spatial planning systems and policies*, European Commission, DG-Regional Policy and Cohesion.

European Commission (1999), *Guidelines for the Assessment of Indirect and Cumulative Impacts as well as Impact Interactions*, Luxemburg: Office for Official Publications of the European Communities.

European Council (2001), Directive 2001/42/EC, *OJ* L 197/30, 21.07.2001.

Fainstein, S.S. and S. Campbell (eds.), (2002), *Readings in Urban Theory* (2nd ed.), Malden, MA: Blackwell Publishing.

Faludi, A. (ed.), (1973a), *A Reader in Planning Theory*, Oxford: Pergamon Press.

Faludi, A. (1973b), *Planning Theory*, Oxford: Pergamon Press.

Faludi, A. (1986), *Critical Rationalism and Planning Methodology*, London: Pion.

Fernández Güell, J.M. (1997), *Planificación Estratégica de Ciudades*, Barcelona: Gustavo Gili.

Fischler, R. (2000), Case Studies of Planners at Work, *Journal of Planning Literature*, **15**(2):184–195.

Flyvbjerg, B. (1998), *Rationality and Power: Democracy in Practice*, Chicago: The University of Chicago Press.

Forrester, J.W. (1961), *Industrial Dynamics*, MIT Press (currently published by Pegasus Communications).

Forrester, J.W. (1969), *Urban Dynamics*, MIT Press (currently published by Pegasus Communications).

Forrester, J.W. (1971), *Principles of Systems*, Wright-Allen Press (currently published by Pegasus Communications).

Friedmann, J. (1967), The Institutional Context, in B.M. Gross (ed.). *Action Under Planning*, New York: McGraw-Hill.

Friedmann, J. (2003), Why do Planning Theory? *Planning Theory*, **2**(1):7–10.

Friend, J., and A. Hickling (2005), *Planning Under Pressure: The Strategic Choice Approach* (3rd ed.), London: Elsevier Butterworth Heineman.

Gezelius, S.S., and K. Refsgaard (2007), Barriers to rational decision-making in environmental planning. *Land Use Policy*, **24**(2):338–348.

Goodstein, L., T. Nolan, and J.W. Pfeiffer (1993), *Applied Strategic Planning: How to Develop a Plan That Really Works*, Boston: McGraw-Hill.

Greed, C. (2000), *Introducing Planning*, London: Athlone Press.

Hall, P. (1992), *Urban and Regional Planning* (3rd ed.), London: Routledge.

Healey, P. (2006), *Collaborative Planning – Shaping Places in Fragmented Societies* (2nd ed.), New York: Palgrave Macmillan.

Healey, P., G. McDougall, and M.J. Thomas (eds), (1982), *Planning Theory – Prospects for the 1980s*, Oxford: Pergamon Press.

Healey, P., G. McDougall, and M.J. Thomas (1982), Theoretical Debates in Planning: Towards a Coherent Dialogue; In: P. Healey, G. McDougall, and M.J. Thomas (eds) *Planning Theory – Prospects for the 1980s*, Oxford: Pergamon Press.

Hempel, C.G, and P. Oppenheim (1948), Studies in the Logic of Explanation, *Philosophy of Science*, **15**(2):135–175.

HMSO (1947), *Town and Country Planning Act*, 10 & 11 Geo. 6, Ch. 53.

Hogarth, R.M., and H. Kunreuther (1995), Decision Making under Ignorance: Arguing with Yourself, *Journal of Risk and Uncertainty*, **10**:15–36.

Hutter, G., and T. Wiechmann (2005), Back to the Future – Emergent Strategies in Strategic Spatial Planning, *Proceedings of the 2005 International Conference of the Regional Studies Association*.

IAIA – International Association for Impact Assessment (2002), *SEA Performance Criteria* Special Publication Series N.1, International Association for Impact Assessment.

IAIA and IEA – International Association for Impact Assessment and Institute of Environmental Assessment (1999), *Principles of EIA Best Practice*, International Association for Impact Assessment in cooperation with the Institute of Environmental Assessment.

Kaplan, R.S., and D.P. Norton (1996), *The Balanced Scorecard: Translating Strategy into Action*, Boston, MA: Harvard Business School Publishing.

Kaplan, R.S., and D.P. Norton (2000), Having Trouble with Your Strategy? Then Map It, *Harvard Business Review*, September-October, R00509.

Kaplan, R.S., and D.P. Norton (2004a), Measuring the Strategic Readiness of Intangible Assets, *Harvard Business Review*, February:1–13.

Kaplan, R.S., and D.P. Norton (2004b), *Strategy Maps: Converting Intangible Assets into Tangible Outcomes*, Boston, MA: Harvard Business School Publishing.

Kelly, E.D., and B. Becker (2000), *Community Planning: An Introduction to the Comprehensive Plan*, Washington DC: Island Press.

King, P.J. (2004), *One Hundred Philosophers – A Guide To The World's Greatest Thinkers*, London: Quarto.

Kørnøv, L., and W.A.H. Thissen (2000), Rationality in decision- and policy-making: implications for strategic environmental assessment, *Impact Assessment and Project Appraisal*, **18**:191–200.

Kuhn, T.S. (1996), *The Structure of Scientific Revolutions* (3rd ed.), Chicago: The University of Chicago Press.

Lacaze, Jean-Paul (1995), *L'Aménagement du Territoire*, Paris: Flammarion.

LGA – Local Government Association (2004), *Research Report 9/04: Skills base in the planning system*, London: LGA.

March, J.G. (1994), *A Primer on Decision Making: How Decisions Happen*, New York: The Free Press.

McCarthy, J. (2004), *Developing Cross-National Learning for Spatial Planning: the Case of Dundee's Overseas Study Visit*, The Geddes Institute, School of Town and Regional Planning, University of Dundee.

McLoughlin, J.B. (1969), *Urban and Regional Planning: a Systems Approach*, London: Faber & Faber.

Minto, B. (2002), *The Pyramid Principle* (3rd ed.), New Jersey: Prentice-Hall.

Mintzberg, H. (1991), Strategy as 'Seeing'; In: J. Nasi (ed.) *Arenas of Strategic Thinking*, Helsinki: Foundation for Economics Education.

Mintzberg, H., B. Ahlstrand, and J. Lampel (1998), *Strategy Safari: a Guided Tour Through the Wilds of Strategic Management*, New York: The Free Press.

Mitchell, B. (1997), *Resource and Environmental Management*, Harlow, Essex: Addison Wesley Longman.

Murray, M. (2004), Strategic Spatial Planning on the Island of Ireland: Towards a New Territorial Logic? *Innovation*, **17**(3):227–242.

Napier, R., C. Sidle, and P. Sanaghan (1998), *High Impact Tools and Activities for Strategic Planning*, New York: McGraw-Hill.

Niven, P.R. (2003), *Balanced Scorecard step-by-step for Government and Non-profit Agencies*, New Jersey: John Wiley & Sons.

OECD (1993), *OECD Core Set of Indicators for Environmental Performance Reviews*, Paris: Organisation for Economic Co-operation and Development.

OECD (2003), *OECD Environmental Indicators: Development, Measurement and Use*, Paris: Organisation for Economic Co-operation and Development.

Okasha, S. (2002), *Philosophy of Science*, Oxford: Oxford University Press.

Osborn, A.F. (1953) *Applied imagination*. Oxford: Scribner.

Perdicoúlis, A. (1997), A Pilot Method for Comparing the Development Alternatives of Syros, Greece, *European Environment*, **7**(5):156–161.

Perdicoúlis, A. (2002a), *Strategic Planning* – in Portuguese, Vila Real: University of Trás-os-Montes e Alto Douro.

Perdicoúlis, A. (2002b), *Strategic Planning Exercises* – in Portuguese, Vila Real: University of Trás-os-Montes e Alto Douro.

Perdicoúlis, A. (2005a), A Structural and Functional Analysis for SEA; In: M. Schmidt, E. João, L. Knopp, and E. Albrecht (eds), *Implementing Strategic Environmental Assessment*, Heidelberg: Springer-Verlag.

Perdicoúlis, A. (2005b), The Urban Planning School of System Dynamics, *WSEAS Transactions on Environment and Development*, **1**(2):173–179.

Perdicoúlis, A. (2008a), Widening the Scope – Sustainability Indicators, Legal Thresholds and Standards in Portugal; In: M. Schmidt, J. Glasson, L. Emmelin and H. Helbron (eds.) *Environmental Impact Assessment – Standards and Thresholds for Human Health and the Environment*, Heidelberg: Springer-Verlag.

Perdicoúlis, A. (2008b), Reverse Blueprinting in a Creative Mode, *The Systems Thinker*, **19**(4):7–9.

Perdicoúlis, A., and B. Durning (2007), An alternating-sequence conceptual framework for EIA-EMS integration, *Journal of Environmental Assessment Policy and Management*, **9**(4):385–397.

Perdicoúlis, A., and J. Glasson (2006), Causal Networks in EIA, *Environmental Impact Assessment Review*, **26**:553–569.

Perdicoúlis, A., and J. Glasson (2007), Action-to-Outcome Maps in Impact Assessment, *The Systems Thinker*, **18**(10):7–10.

Perdicoúlis, A., and J. Glasson (2009), The causality premise of EIA in practice, *Impact Assessment and Project Appraisal*, **27**(3):247–250.

Perdicoúlis, A., and J. Piper (2008), Network and system diagrams revisited: satisfying CEA requirements for causality analysis, *Environmental Impact Assessment Review*, **28**:455–468.

Perdicoúlis, A., and S. Power (1995), Environmental Constraints to the Economic and Social Development of Small Islands, *European Environment*,

5(3):76–81.

Perdicoúlis, A., M. Hanusch, H.D. Kasperidus, and U. Weiland (2007), The Handling of Causality in SEA Guidance, *Environmental Impact Assessment Review*, **27**:176–187.

Perloff, H.S. (1957), *Education for Planning: City, State, & Regional*, Westport, CT: Greeenwood Press.

Plato (360 BC), *The Republic*, translated by B. Jowett, published by Project Gutenberg, www.gutenberg.org/.

Reade, E. (1983), If Planning is Anything, Maybe it Can be Identified, *Urban Studies*, **20**:159–171.

Reid, D. (1995), *Sustainable Development: an Introductory Guide*, London: Earthscan.

Richardson, T. (2005), Environmental assessment and planning theory: four short stories about power, multiple rationality, and ethics, *Environmental Impact Assessment Review*, **25**:341–365.

Roberts, M. (1974), *An Introduction to Town Planning Techniques*, London: Hutchinson.

RTPI – Royal Town Planning Institute (2003), *Introductory Guide to Planning & Environmental Protection*, London: RTPI.

Sager, T. (1998), Public Planning and Arrow's Theorem, *Progress in Planning*, **50**:75–140.

Sartorio, F.S. (2005), Strategic Spatial Planning: A Historical Review of Approaches, its Recent Revival, and an Overview of the State of the Art in Italy, *disP*, **162**:26–40.

Scriven, M. (1959), Explanation and Prediction in Evolutionary Theory, *Science*, **130**(3374):477–482.

Scriven, M. (1975), Causation as Explanation, *Noûs*, **9**(1):3–16.

Senge, P.M. (1990), *The Fifth Discipline: The Art and Practice of the Learning Organization*, New York: Doubleday.

Senge, P.M. (2006), *The Fifth Discipline: The Art and Practice of the Learning Organization* (2nd ed.), London: Random House.

Senge, P.M., A. Kleiner, C. Roberts, R.B. Ross, and B.J. Smith (1994), *The Fifth Discipline Fieldbook: Strategies and Tools for Building a Learning Organization*, London: Nicholas Brealey Publishing.

Shafir, E., and A. Tversky (1992), Thinking through Uncertainty: Nonconsequential Reasoning and Choice, *Cognitive Psychology*, **24**:449–474.

Simon, H.A. (1957), *Models of Man*, New York: John Wiley and Sons.

Smith, S.P., and W.R. Sheate (2001), Sustainability Appraisal of English Regional Plans: Incorporating the Requirements of the EU Strategic Environmental Assessment Directive, *Impact Assessment and Project Appraisal*, **19**(4):263–276.

Sterman, J.D. (2000), *Business Dynamics*, Boston: Irwin McGraw-Hill.

Stoeglehner, G. (2004), Integrating Strategic Environmental Assessment into Community Development Plans – a Case Study from Austria, *European Environment*, **14**(2):58–72.

Taylor, N. (1998), *Urban Planning Theory since 1945*, London: Sage.

Thérivel, R., and M.R. Partidário (1996), *The Practice of Strategic Environmental Assessment*, London: Earthscan.

Thomas, H. (2004), What Future for British Planning Theory, *Planning Theory*, **3**(3):189–198.

Tsivakou, I. (1996), The written form of planning, *Scandinavian Journal of Management*, **12**:69–88.

Turner, T. (1998), *Landscape Planning and Environmental Impact Design* (2nd ed.), London: UCL Press.

US ACE – United States Army Corps of Engineers (1996), *Planning Manual*, IWR Report 96-R-21.

van Groenendaal, W.J.H. (2003), Group decision support for public policy planning, *Information & Management*, **40**:371–380.

Vennix, J.A.M., 1996, Group Model Building: Facilitating Team Learning Using System Dynamics, Chichester: John Wiley & Sons.

Vigar, G., P. Healey, A. Hull, and S. Davoudi (2000), *Planning, Governance and Spatial Strategy in Britain*, Basingstoke, Hampshire: Macmillan Press.

Wandersman, A., P. Imm, M. Chinman, and S. Kaftarian (2000), Getting to Outcomes: a results-based approach to accountability, *Evaluation and Program Planning*, **23**:389–395.

Wates, N. (2000), *The Community Planning Handbook*, London: Earthscan.

Wong, C. (1998), Old Wine in a New Bottle? Planning Methods and Techniques in the 1990s, *Planning Practice and Research*, **13**(3):221–236.

Wootton, S., and T. Horne (1997), *Strategic Thinking: A Step-By-Step Approach to Strategy*, London: Kogan Page.

Yeang, K. (1999), *Proyectar con la Naturaleza – Bases Ecológicas para el Proyecto Arquitectónico*, Barcelona: Editorial Gustavo Gili.

Yewlett, C.J.L. (2001), OR in strategic land-use planning, *Journal of the Operational Research Society*, **52**:4–13.

Index